The Emperor's Cupboard

More clarity and impact for business leaders
through Western psychology and Eastern wisdom

Thomas Gartenmann, Ph.D.

The Emperor's Cupboard

More clarity and impact for business leaders
through Western psychology and Eastern wisdom

Thomas Gartenmann, Ph.D.

The Swirling Leaf Press

The Swirling Leaf Press

www.swirlingleafpress.com
info@swirlingleafpress.com

The psychological explanations and models used within the book have appeared in the *Transformations Perspectives Series*' at www.aergon.com and in three articles at https://morethandigital.info/. The exercises, accessible via the links at the end of relevant chapters, have been carefully prepared and tested in the context of facilitated workshops, however no guarantee can be given on their outcome in other contexts. Neither the author nor the publisher accept liability for damages of any kind.

Book design and images by Bernd Altenried www.almo.de

Translated from German to English by Guthrun Love www.lovelanguage.co.nz

Edited by Rachna Chowla and Verónica Fajardo www.swirlingleafpress.com

Published in London, United Kingdom

ISBN 978-1-915766-00-7

To our children,
and the inner child in us all

'If I am not for myself, who will be for me?
If I am not for others, what am I?
And if not now, when?'

Hillel

Introduction: the journey that led me here

To anyone looking in from the outside in the mid-1990s, I seemed to have it all – I had several advanced degrees under my belt that had led me onto a career that many would find impressive, and I had a happy family life. To crown it all, I had just been appointed a Partner & Managing Director at the Boston Consulting Group (BCG). For a brief time, I felt I was on top of the world. This feeling ,however, did not last long and what happened next shook me to my core, but was also the start of an enriching journey of personal and professional growth, which continues to this day and forms the basis of this book.

After the initial honeymoon period as a Partner was over, my new position at BCG began to make me feel increasingly pressured. I internalised this and began to feel inadequate in myself and unable to meet others' expectations. Not only did I feel that I was not good enough, but there was also a deeper layer of anger, directed at myself, because I believed that I had not worked hard enough and that if I had, things would be better. My days at work felt fraught and my nights at home too – I would lay awake, helplessly prey to a tumultuous storm of thoughts of worry and anxiety, feeling real dread for the next day.

Only later, after much reflection, did I realise that this way of thinking was the result of a much earlier conditioning, and that all along I had been unconsciously heading towards this culmination point. As a child, I had often been led to feel that I wasn't 'good enough'. What's more, during my young adult life, I had scarcely acknowledged my emotions, let alone given them space to evolve. As a result, my coping mechanisms were limited to this – I wanted to prove my value through extreme commitment. I was friendly to everyone and I suppressed the healthy anger I felt when my feelings were hurt. In my sphere of learning, I had focused exclusively on professional, technical competencies and avoided anything vaguely emotional. Back then, as a management consultant, we were thrown straight into the deep end and expected to gain expert knowledge directly and quickly through client projects, supplemented by internal training. The possibility of seeking support to deal with personal and professional challenges in the form of coaching was only mentioned privately in hushed tones, if at all.

But I was lucky. I found a coach, and not only did he help me through this difficult time with his valuable input, but after a few months he even suggested that I undertake a two-year training course to become a coach myself. He felt I would learn and benefit even more from a group of like-minded people. At the time, given my sense of self and a very busy job, I found this suggestion quite bizarre. Was I really ready to take on something like this? And in addition to everything else? How was I supposed to find the time? I said yes anyway, and it turned out to be the beginning of an exciting and fulfilling journey of inner discovery, which allowed me to flourish in my work at BCG and support my colleagues in doing the same.

Later in my journey, I drew additional support from three other areas that feature heavily in this book – my interest in Eastern wisdom and practices such as meditation, my passion for stories, and integrating these within the context of modern-day psychology. Meditation has made me more aware of my inner processes and enabled me to gain a more nuanced understanding of the genesis of my thoughts and feelings. This, in turn, has enabled me to be aware of more during my encounters with other people, both within myself and within others. Eastern or Zen stories and parables have throughout the years prompted me to reflect on and question my beliefs and attitudes. In addition came the learning from life's challenges, from leading ambitious projects at BCG, having open conversations with friends and colleagues, not least my wife and my three children, who provided a safe and loving space for me to develop, practise and hone the techniques described in this book.

For me, undertaking this journey has helped me engage better with the many and varied challenges that life brings. I have experienced the benefits, both physical and mental, that can be gained from meditation, reflection and having a greater understanding of psychology. I am more at ease and relaxed within myself, yet I feel more invigorated. I feel a deep and strong connection with the people around me – my family, my colleagues and my community. Learning from these experiences, together with the Zen stories that I have been collecting for many years and my deep interest in psychology, has given birth to this book – a book about leadership which I wish I could have read at the start of my career.

The title of this book, *The Emperor's Cupboard*, comes from a Zen story with the same name featured in Chapter 9. The story is about the thought processes and inner obstacles we might encounter when we plan to bring something new into the world. As you will read, the master craftsman in the story, who is also a Zen monk, saw and overcame various obstacles within himself through his meditation. Only after this was he able to build the most magnificent cupboard for the emperor, something I have not yet been able to apply with the same effect while writing this book.

What is this book about?

This book is about discovering more about who you are. Or, more precisely, it invites you to enquire into what it is that makes you *you* and what will make you more impactful in your own life – in your relationship with yourself (self-impact) and also in your relationship with others, especially those that you lead as a business leader.

By combining insights from modern-day psychology with stories of a special kind, Zen stories, which have been passed down over centuries, you are invited to gain a deeper understanding of yourself. In doing so, you can also learn how to deal with the challenges that surround you in a calmer, more productive way.

Many **Eastern traditions**, including Zen Buddhism, refer to a way of being that does not allow itself to be captured and defined in words or concepts. They are not a doctrine you are supposed to believe in, nor are they an intellectual net you can use to catch the fish of reality. Instead, they describe the water that flows through every net and which almost always escapes our grasp. The only way to be more aware of this watery medium is to learn to swim in it, to dive in and allow yourself to be moved by the currents, and to enjoy its dynamic power and effect.

The misshaped circle that appears on the cover of this book is the Ensō, a sacred and ancient Zen symbol. It is a circle, hand-drawn with a single, uninhibited brushstroke. It symbolises an array of concepts, from the Universe, to the beginning and the end of all things, enlightenment, and ultimately the interconnectedness of existence. It also plays with the idea of perfection and imperfection, seemingly perfect in its continuity and balance, yet irregular in its shape and form, hence also serving as an expression of the present moment.

> Psychology gives us insights into how, in our complex world, we can forge a more inspired and fulfilling path for ourselves to walk.

The discipline of **psychology** can also help us to better understand our human existence and to accept it with greater equanimity. In contrast with Zen Buddhism, psychology is a young science that can also shed light on our human desires and aspirations, both conscious, and more importantly, unconscious. It enables us to understand what it is that defines our human condition and also gives us insights into how, in our complex world, we can forge a more inspiring and fulfilling path for ourselves to walk.

As a business leader, a large part of your job, and one which requires sensitivity, is how you lead your employees through change. It is employees who most often feel the increasing variety of challenge and stress of disruptive change. So, how can you, as a leader, help others deal with change, which in today's world involves volatility, uncertainty, complexity and ambiguity (VUCA)? In this VUCA world there is a real danger that employees can see themselves as victims of circumstance beyond their control, or as pawns to be sacrificed, in the throes of change programmes and innovations, naturally prompting feelings of insecurity, stress and resistance.

This book is about supporting you as a leader to become more aware of your own internal processes (your own mental map) and to change them if needed, so that you think, feel and act from a place of greater clarity and equanimity, enabling you to then better lead and support your employees, especially when navigating change and business transformation.

How is the book structured?

The opening chapter describes the contours of an inner psychological map, which we will explore and fill in further in this book. The subsequent three chapters focus on the psychological constructs that we acquire, generally unconsciously, during the course of our socialisation. These are constructs that once had a useful purpose but may now have become a hindrance to **more clarity**. These include our coping mechanisms, our drivers and attitudes, and ultimately our identity, all of which at times can inhibit our ability to be present in the here and now. These chapters can support you, the 'I', to become more aware and to integrate more of these unconscious parts within yourself.

Chapter 5 introduces the idea of collective attitudes, the 'WE', that also contributes to our sense of identity. Chapter 6 then discusses the concept of polarities, a key idea which is also touched upon in the previous chapter on values. Chapter 7 further develops this perspective and explores the elements required for leading a meaningful life, both at home and at work.

Chapters 8 to 10 explore how to forge a personal connection to a company or organisation and present the core aspects of leadership with reference to the I, WE and IT dimensions (the 'IT' dimension being the external world), enabling you to create **more impact**.

Chapter 11, the final chapter, completes the Ensō circle of this book by illustrating how awareness and personal presence can lead to deeper connection and impact in interpersonal relationships and communication.

How might you wish to read this book?

First, the most direct route between two points is seldom the best path to take. By taking detours and exploring side roads, you will often reach your goal more quickly, or at least with a greater sense of fulfilment. While the chapters in this book follow a linear plan and can be read in sequence, each chapter can also stand on its own. So, if the impulse arises, take the opportunity to take some detours in this book. Similarly, the exercises do not need to be done in any particular order either.

Second, nothing that is written here is true. A statement only acquires truth if it resonates with you. This book invites you to embark on this journey with an attitude of 'shoshin (初心)'. In Zen, *shoshin* stands for an attitude we can translate as 'beginner's mind'. It means approaching a new subject with an attitude of curiosity, open-mindedness, and without prejudice – as a child or beginner would, even if you, the student, are coming from a more advanced level. And this brings us to our first Zen story:

> *Nan-in[1], a Zen master, received a visit from a university professor who wanted to understand Zen. No sooner had he arrived than the professor began to ask questions and to expound his own theories. Meanwhile, Nan-in served him tea. He poured the tea until the visitor's cup was full, and then he kept on pouring. The professor watched the cup overflowing until he could no longer contain himself, 'Can't you see it's full? There's no room for any more!' 'Just like this cup,' replied Nan-in, 'You are full of your own ideas and opinions. If you want me to show you Zen, first you must empty your own cup.'*

Or to quote Gabriel García Márquez, who expressed this radical openness towards life in a single poignant sentence, 'I love my wife so much that I don't know who she is!'

1 Nan-in was a Japanese Zen master from the Meiji era (19th century).

What might you want to get from this book?

In my experience as a coach, having clarity about an intention[2] is helpful in all processes, including reading this book – perhaps you would like some tips on how to be more aware and to find more satisfaction in your life, as well as your work? Or maybe you are seeking an answer to a particular challenge? It's up to you to determine your own specific reason.

What if you want to delve deeper into these topics and put what you have learned into practice?

When you have an insight or a discovery, I invite you to be curious and playful about it and see where trying to implement it takes you. If you need more structured help, at the end of most chapters you will find some supportive exercises that you can access by activating a link or QR code. **In addition, you can find the Zen stories in a podcast on Spotify or Amazon, where I discuss their meaning with friends.** Lastly, the final chapter is dedicated entirely to real-life communication practice and the ongoing practical application of the insights you have gained.

2 From the Latin verb *intendere*, which means to focus your endeavours on a particular goal.

Chapter 1

Mapping the contours of your mental landscape, the place where change begins

The nun and the well

One day, some people came to see a hermit nun. They asked, 'What purpose do you find in your life of silence and meditation?' The nun was busy drawing water from a deep well as she said to her visitors, 'Look in the well. What do you see?' The people looked into the deep well and replied, 'We can't see anything!'

After a while, the nun again instructed her visitors, 'Look in the well! What do you see now?' The people looked down again into the well, 'Now we can see ourselves!'

The nun then said, 'Before, the water was disturbed because I was drawing up the bucket. Now the water is calm. That is what you experience through silence and meditation, you are able to see yourself! Now wait a while longer.' After a while, the nun said again, 'Now look in the well. What do you see?'

The people looked down, and replied, 'Now we can see the stones at the bottom of the well.'

The nun explained, 'That is what you experience through silence and meditation. If you give yourself a lot of time and a lot of space, you can see through to the bottom of all things.'

Questions to reflect on

› *From the nun's point of view, what is the purpose of meditation?*

› *What is the 'bottom of all things' in relation to people?*

› *What does that mean to you in a figurative sense?*

› *When it comes to dealing with stress, do you just live with your usual way of dealing with it, or do you try to change or improve how you respond?*

For some hints about potential answers to these questions, see the text on the next page.
They may offer a 'change of perspective'.

From the nun's point of view, what is the purpose of meditation?

The water well functions as a metaphor to illustrate the effect of meditation. Through stillness and conscious awareness, we can perceive our inner processes – the sensations, feelings, thoughts and intentions that we have, in a more nuanced way – as they form and arise, and as they disappear. This enables us to recognise a greater range of possibilities and to make decisions more consciously, i.e., to come up with an answer that is appropriate to the situation, instead of simply reacting instinctively. We cannot see ourselves fully without calm reflection and we cannot understand others and see fully how and why they respond without first understanding ourselves.

What is 'the bottom of all things' in relation to people?

This refers to a state of pure consciousness that is impossible to describe, but easier to experience through meditation.

External pressures at work and in our private lives have increased significantly and we often react to them in a predetermined way, which may be irritable, dismissive, or angry, or we may feel overwhelmed and withdraw away feeling hurt. It is mostly the same stressors that trigger the same reactions. **So, when it comes to dealing with stress, do you just live with your usual way of dealing with it, or do you try to change or improve how you respond?**

Even the way that you engaged with this first exercise reveals something about you – did you take your time to reflect on the questions, or did you turn straight to the answers? Do not judge yourself about either choice, just notice.

'We may not be responsible for the world that created our minds, but we can take responsibility for the mind with which we create our world.'

Gabor Maté

The story of the nun at the water well shows how meditation leads to inner clarity. When I first started meditating, it was still a rather unusual endeavour, and at the time, even esoteric for some. Today, in addition to the scientifically proven and well documented benefits for the body and mind, meditation is seen as an excellent way to increase the quality of thought processes, perception and focus, thus making life more conscious (Boccia et al. 2015). There are countless books, courses, groups and apps that offer instructions for meditation. In my coaching work, I often recommend the 'Waking up – Unlocking your mind' app as a good introduction to meditation.

The number of companies that now offer meditation courses for their employees shows how highly accepted it has become in the corporate world. The focus, however, should not be on the obvious benefits or 'side-effects' of meditation, but rather on the direct experience of 'being' as opposed to 'doing'. Only when I direct my attention to my inner self, taking an inner 'screenshot' of my physical, emotional and mental experiences in the moment, do I become aware of my inner state. If I now use a few deeper breaths to sink a little deeper, I am already in meditation. The story of the nun illustrates the 'clear seeing' that can emerge with meditation[3].

But what role does psychology have here? What about the clear seeing that can come from the 'mental maps' that we use to operate in the world? For well over a century, the terrain of our entire planet has been captured in detailed maps, and today, with the aid of satellite photos and GPS, we can find our way around virtually anywhere in the world. As human beings, we also carry around with us an internal map of the world, which we use to generate our own personal explanations of the phenomena around us. While we are constantly updating this map with new information, we rarely redraw it from scratch. This idea of a 'map of the human psyche' is a useful model which can offer you some important points of reference on your own personal 'mental map'.

3 You can use the promo code OPENMIND to get a free month's subscription to Sam Harris' Waking up app available at www.wakingup.com

As Alfred Korzybski (1933) aptly put it, 'A map is not the territory it represents, but, if correct, it has a similar structure to the territory, which accounts for its usefulness.' Although a suitable map offers us the possibility of finding our way, we must remember that it is an abstract construct and so not fall into the trap of confusing the map with the territory itself. In our case, we must not confuse our mental maps with the much more profound and diverse world of experience, especially as our mental maps are always influenced by our feelings[4]. Only once we are aware of this we can learn to understand the emotional likes and dislikes that we have unconsciously developed and which drive our decisions, and so clearly see how to express them in a more conscious way.

According to BCG, only 25% of all projects aimed at implementing change within a company achieve their stated goals (Fæste et al., 2014). Why is that? When companies want to change, in general, they focus on the corporate structure and on adapting the organisation, processes, guidelines, systems, technologies, etc. But what is perhaps more important and all too often overlooked (or ignored) is the internal or inner transformation needed within those involved in the change process – of their feelings, thoughts, and attitudes, i.e., their mental maps, towards the change process. Because it is inner transformation in thinking, feeling and acting that gives life to any strategy.

For something to change on the outside, the relevant change must first take place inside those people that are involved. This process requires behavioural change, which in part involves our unconscious psychological processes, both as individuals and collectively. It is no wonder then that this kind of process takes time and sensitivity. Let's start by taking a look in the mirror: *How successful have you been in the last few years at making behavioural changes in your personal life? For example, in doing more exercise, spending more time with your family, keeping up with hobbies, eating more healthily, being less stressed and so on.* If you admit to not being 'very successful' in this department, the next question would be why? What were the reasons? And almost everyone will have some difficulty in answering this question.

4 In Zen, there is a principle called *Place no trust in words*. This means that words alone cannot express the essence of Zen as words and concepts fragment reality and stop movement.

This reflection perhaps reveals the challenge inherent in every attempt to implement change in a team, department, or company. *If we do not really understand our own change psychology (which suggests that we have not been able to cultivate our awareness about this phenomenon), we are unlikely to be able to successfully bring about change in our employees.*

This, among other reasons, is why it is critically important to convey the **purpose** behind the change to all those involved at the earliest possible stage, or better still, to co-develop the shared purpose behind the change with them in the first instance. This gives rise to the need for structural processes to closely involve the people concerned so that they feel they are connected with and are part of the process. Studies have also shown that people are more likely to be willing to engage with a task if they feel it is meaningful, as this increases motivation and satisfaction and reduces stress (Lips-Wiersma & Wright, 2012). And of course, all of these contribute to an individual's general sense of well-being. Then, intentionally creating a work environment that employees experience as meaningful is in the interests of both the employees and the company. For leaders in particular, aligning their own quest for purpose with the **company's purpose** is crucial in order to be successful in their role, but this is especially true in change situations.

The man on the horse

A man sits on his horse as it gallops off at speed, giving the impression that he must be on his way to a very important meeting. Another man is standing at the side of the road and calls out to him, 'Where are you going?' to which the rider replies, 'I have no idea. Ask the horse!'

We can apply this story to our daily lives, both at work and at home. We are like the rider on his horse, we do not always know where we're going, but neither do we know how to stop, so we just carry on galloping further and further down the road. In this way, we can become victims of circumstance.

We explore purpose later on, in Chapter 7. For now, we will start by looking at change, in particular the **unconscious, psychological aspects** of it. We will do so taking into account the different levels that exist within a company that is going through a transformation – the 'I' individual level and the collective 'WE' level, and we will see how to bring these two together.

A clear distinction should be made between the meaning inherent in the terms **change** and **transformation** for the purposes of this book:

› Change takes place in the external world, or at the 'IT' level

› Transformation is an internal, irreversible shift in a person's understanding and core perspectives, and this takes place in the 'I' and 'WE' dimensions[5].

A change process, when understood in a holistic sense, comprises the following dimensions:

› Inner recognition and alignment

› External implementation

› Individual level

› Collective level

5 The quintessential metaphor for transformation is the metamorphosis of a caterpillar into a butterfly. At first glance, this appears to be an external transformation. But, funnily enough, because of the way its eyes are positioned, the butterfly is unable to see its transformed self. The real transformation is on the inside; all the 'very hungry' caterpillar can do is wriggle along a two-dimensional surface and fill its stomach with green leaves. The butterfly, on the other hand, can fly freely through three-dimensional space – experiencing a new perspective and taking a sip of nectar from time to time.

These can be combined with a matrix developed by Ken Wilber, an American philosopher and pioneering thinker in philosophy, as shown in figure 1:

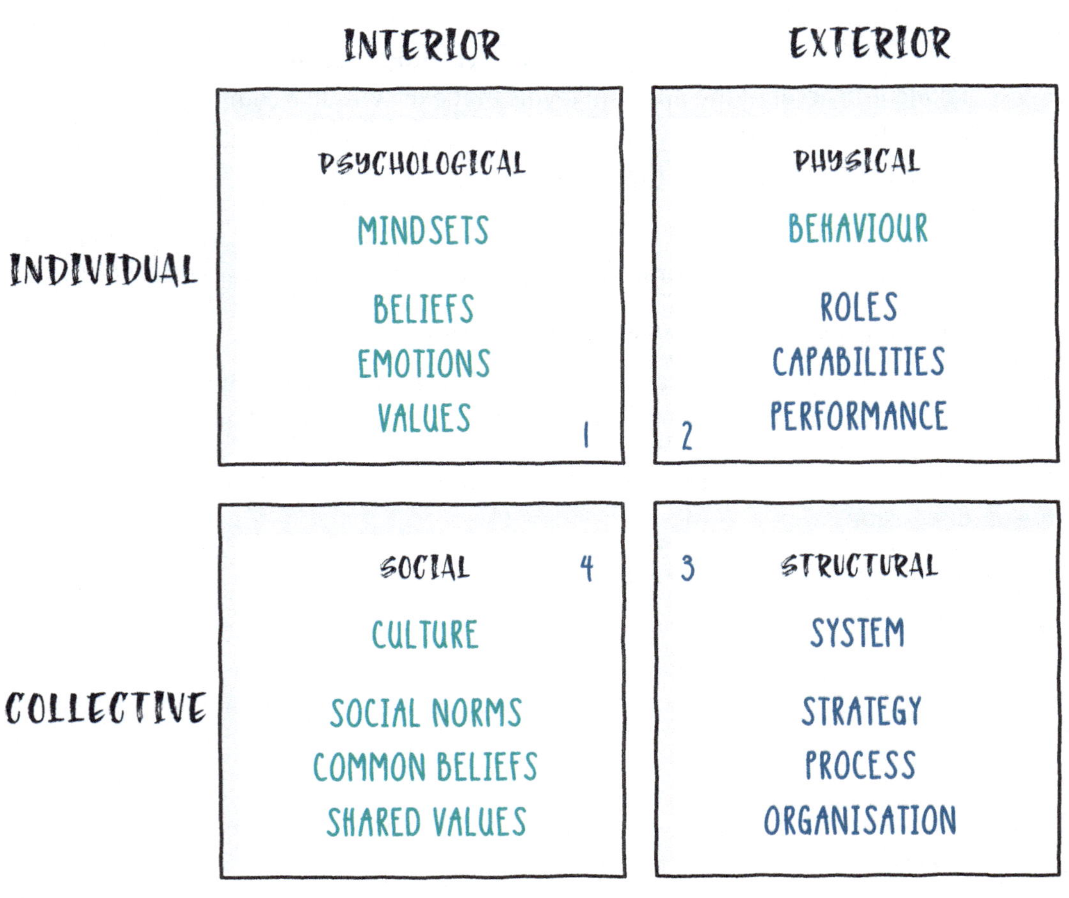

Figure 1: Inside-out/Outside-in matrix (Ken Wilber, 2011)

This matrix gives us some clear markers on our mental map and some starting points for a successful holistic change process in a company, which intentionally takes account of the need for transformation at various levels. As a leader, it is important to:

- **Align your behaviour with your mindset (the 'I' level), i.e., to be aware of your own values and beliefs, and to intentionally align your behaviour with them (moving from quadrant 1 to 2)**
  Acting as a role model for the desired behaviour is significantly more effective than simply telling someone to change their behaviour. This is supported by two distinct leadership elements that we will investigate in future chapters, the ability to openly discuss cultural expectations, and the willingness to engage in constructive conflict, with a view to resolution, when met with resistance.
- **Nurture a culture where individual mindsets align and support collective values and beliefs (the collective 'WE' level), because purpose and ways of working have been jointly developed over time (moving from quadrant 1 to 4)**
  When values and ways of working are co-developed within a team and the broader organisation in a meaningful way, a culture of trust is naturally created, which enables the plasticity for change and high-performance within teams.
- **Lastly, support the co-creation of the necessary strategy, process and structural adjustments to achieve the co-defined change (moving from quadrant 4 to 3, and from 1 to 2).**

In every conversation and interaction with our employees, we can apply these insights and share our current understanding in a more coherent and mindful manner[6]. The focus of this book is on helping you become more aware of your self-impact and socio-cultural competence, and strengthening these further (quadrants 1 and 4).

Having drawn these first rough lines of a mental map, you are now ready to embark upon a journey through the following chapters and fill in any gaps with new insights and experiences.

Conclusion

- **Most of our decisions** and actions are **unconscious**.
- In any transformation, the first step is to recognise and **become aware of our drivers and our orientation.**
- **'Transformation' is an internal process which takes place in the 'I' and 'WE' dimensions.** 'Change' refers to an external change to the structure and processes and takes place in the 'IT' dimension.
- **Meditation** is an excellent way to **become more aware** of the inner emotional, physical and mental experiences happening in the moment.

---

6 A connection is often drawn between this kind of transformation and what happens when you leave your comfort zone and take the plunge into your learning zone. However, the comfort zone is a misnomer. It suggests we are comfortable there, but this zone represents the sum of all our conscious and unconscious habits, so it feels familiar, but this does not necessarily mean that we feel comfortable - it can often feel quite uncomfortable! So, it might better be thought of as a 'familiarity' zone, rather than a 'comfort' zone.

Chapter 2

Individual thought systems and stress triggers

The monk and the young woman

Two monks were going on a long journey. One day, they came to the bank of a wide river. A young woman stood there, dressed in beautiful, costly clothes. Obviously, she wanted to cross the river, but she was hesitating because the water was very deep and she didn't want to ruin her clothes.

The elder of the two monks went up to the young woman, lifted her up and waded through the water with her on his shoulders. He set her down on the bank on the other side.

After the younger monk had also crossed the river, they both continued their journey, but anger began to brew in the younger monk. Sometime later, he started to criticise the older monk, 'That was wrong of you. We are forbidden to have any contact with women, or even speak to them. And you went so far as to even touch her. Why did you break this rule?'

The elder monk listened thoughtfully to these reproaches. Then he answered calmly, 'I only carried the woman across the river. You've carried her all the way here.'

Questions to reflect on

› *What is it that determines the attitudes and beliefs of the two monks?*

› *What exactly did the young monk carry with him, i.e., what was it that he was unable to let go of?*

› *What is it that gives rise to these two different attitudes towards the same event?*

› *Can you think of something you've been unable or unwilling to let go of?*

› *What areas of your life are in standby mode? And what areas are in growth mode?*

What is it that determines the attitudes and beliefs of the two monks?

The two monks have different value and belief systems that lead them to assess the situation in a different way. The young monk adheres strictly to the rules he has learned and internalised, while the older monk sees a person in distress, feels empathy for her and shows compassion; he is present and able to act in the moment, unfettered by the past or by the rules of his community.

What exactly did the young monk carry with him, i.e., what was it that he was unable to let go of?

The young monk's internalisation of the rules draws him into a conflict between what he has accepted as the rule and holds to be right, and the divergent behaviour of the older monk. Because he cannot resolve this inner conflict, it keeps simmering inside him and he carries it around with him until he cannot help but externalise it by reproaching the older monk.

What is it that gives rise to these two different attitudes towards the same event?

The different attitudes arise from two different levels of awareness that evolve depending on whether we live life according to a fixed set of rules that give structure to the world and prescribe what is right and wrong (and which provide a sense of clarity and security), or whether we live in the present moment and can make decisions based on the immediate situation.

'The heart has its reasons which reason knows nothing of... We know the truth not only by the reason, but by the heart.'

Blaise Pascal

Barely a century ago, we had no way of understanding what it is that defined a person's inner being. According to Sigmund Freud, the father of psychoanalysis, a person's psychological dimension was, at best, an accident of the unconscious mind. This same mystery shrouded the origins of a person's motives, attitudes and feelings. Today, thanks to advances in fields such as cognitive neuroscience and behavioural economics, we know a bit more about these phenomena. A vital contribution came from the research of psychologist Daniel Kahneman, whose work gained him, together with Vernon Smith, the Nobel Memorial Prize in Economic Sciences in 2002. Kahneman realised that humans have **two different thought systems** which govern our perceptions and understanding. These two systems can sometimes lead us to making contradictory decisions – a phenomenon which was previously dismissed simply as irrational behaviour. Kahneman (2011) describes:

In reality we exercise much less conscious control over our decisions than we generally assume and our cognitive abilities are scarcely more developed than those of our ancient ancestors.

- **System 1** as being fast, automatic, constantly active, adept at forming emotional stereotypes, and **unconscious**
- **System 2** as slow, taking a lot of energy, only occasionally active, logical, calculating, and **conscious**.

In stressful situations, it is the unconscious System 1 that tends to have the strongest influence on our decision-making. And as long as we remain unaware of this state of quasi-automatism to which we are conditioned, we are unknowingly on autopilot.

What does this insight mean for our everyday lives? First, it means that we exercise much less conscious control over our decisions than we assume. In addition, our cognitive abilities, in which we trust almost blindly, are scarcely more developed than those of our ancient ancestors. In a series of experiments, Kahneman and his team demonstrated that in terms of our own perceptions, as human beings we have a tendency towards distorted understanding, overly simplified solutions, and an exaggerated estimation of our own abilities.

From a purely evolutionary perspective, our brain has three parts that have evolved over millions of years: a primitive reptilian part, a more developed emotional mammalian part, and finally, the more logical primate part. While all three parts are connected, they often act independently, or even push us in different directions. If we bring this knowledge of evolutionary biology together with Kahneman's insights from cognitive science, a pattern emerges:

› It becomes clear that System 1 belongs to the reptilian and mammalian parts of our brain
› System 2 belongs to the primate part, which is cognitively the most developed

Under ideal circumstances, all three parts of the brain work together in harmony. But as soon as we are put under pressure, the two evolutionarily older parts take control. The same happens when we fall head over heels in love. As a result, we switch to survival (and reproduction) mode. This is also because of the amygdala, an almond-shaped structure that forms part of the limbic system in the mammalian part of the brain. The limbic system is where emotions are processed and the amygdala is specifically responsible for feelings of fear. As soon as we feel we're in danger, the amygdala takes over, instructing the adrenal gland to serve us a heady hormone cocktail of adrenaline, followed later by cortisol. While this may not actually make us drunk, it does severely limit our ability to act rationally. One of the things that these so-called stress hormones do is switch off most of the frontal cortex, which is the logical part of the primate brain. This situation is often referred to as an 'amygdala hijack', where our capacity for rational thought is literally hijacked by that part of our brain. This 'fight or flight' response makes sense in critical survival-type situations requiring an immediate reaction, where there is simply no time to stop and reflect on the situation. But in a modern-day office environment, what may have been essential for the survival of our ancestors in the wild can come across as an illogical or irrational reaction, perhaps perceived by others as even over-the-top. We can respond to situations that seem stressful to us in a more appropriate way if we know how to handle - to regulate - overwhelming emotions[7].

---

7 Edward O. Wilson, Professor of Entomology and Evolutionary Biology, expressed it succinctly, 'The real problem of humanity is the following: We have Paleolithic emotions, medieval institutions and godlike technology.'

The term 'stress', which we all use so often, is by definition the psychological and/or physical response to an external stimulus. This response can be fight, flight or freeze and once triggered, this automatic physiological reaction has to run its course, i.e., it is almost irreversible[8]. Frequent, intense or inappropriate activation of this type of stress response is implicated in various clinical conditions including anxiety. So, for our long-term well-being, especially given the challenges we face at work, it is important not to switch to survival mode every time we sense danger. Instead, we need to learn how to deal with stress more consciously. This requires that we recognise that the way our brain evaluates potential stress triggers is **unique to each of us** – in other words, we all find different things stressful. So, if we cannot change *our stress response*, it should be possible to at least raise the stimulus threshold before such a response is triggered in us. Our goal is to re-interpret these stimuli so we can deal with them in a different way.

Whatever our different stress triggers and however many of them we have, they are mostly established during childhood. At that point in our lives, they represented the most intelligent response our system could generate when dealing with external challenges. It is not so much the actual events from our childhood that determine what triggers our stress response as adults, but rather the quality of our relationships with our caregivers during the first years of childhood, and the ability of these important people in our lives to recognise our emotions and to regulate them appropriately[9]. If we did not feel safe and protected as children, or form any lasting relationships, or were not given any guidance, if our potential was not recognised and encouraged, or if we were not loved – these are a recipe for all kinds of trauma. And developmental traumas such as these, are not just something that happened back in the distant past, they are something that leave an enduring impression on our mind, brain and body (van der Kolk, 2014). Unhealed trauma prevents us from being present in the moment, which limits our ability to engage with others and to act appropriately in a given situation.

---

8 Stephen W. Porges, Professor of Psychiatry, has studied the response patterns of our autonomic nervous system and described them in detail in his polyvagal theory. This theory also explains how an individual's sense of safety or danger is deeply intertwined with their social environment. Our brains develop sequentially from the bottom up, and our experiences are processed in the same way. This means that the most primitive, reactive part of our brain (System 1) is the first part to interpret and react to incoming information from our senses. Hence, our brains will act and feel before we think.

9 Research has shown that attachment styles which individuals develop during childhood, as a result of their interactions with their caregivers, will be similar to the attachment styles exhibited in their adult romantic relationships (Hazan & Shaver, 1987). For an assessment of your personal attachment style see the exercise section.

Even in the 21st century, we still face the challenge of outwitting our reptilian and mammalian brains to avoid the emotional traps we are conditioned to fall into. The first step in this direction is to be aware of the personal red buttons that trigger a stress response in us. Even if this does not enable us to change our behaviour straight away, afterwards we can at least reflect on what happened, and what we could have done differently. What would have been a better, more prudent response?

A couple of tried and tested 'emergency techniques' for coping with stressful situations are to step back and take a panoramic view, and to consciously regulate our breathing – these are both physiological processes that we can control[10]. The next step is to give precise names to the emotions we are experiencing. This can help us to break out of the automated response that is unleashed by the stress trigger, and next time we may recognise the emotion earlier and consciously intervene a little earlier too, ultimately reconditioning our responses.

Keeping our emotions under control at the right time is certainly a worthwhile aspiration for us all. But for us as leaders, this ability is a key requirement in our everyday work. The responsibility inherent to being a leader means being frequently exposed to stressful situations where an ill-considered primitive response driven by panic might not only have unpleasant consequences for us, but also push a series of red buttons amongst our employees. Stressed employees are not just unhappy, often the stress they experience also prevents them from generating their desired creativity and innovation.

Learning to recognise our own stress triggers[11] is a relatively easy exercise when we are not stressed compared to trying to notice them in the moment, when they are already triggering a stress response, and we are trying to cope and choose a more situationally appropriate behaviour. In practice, we use a lot of different words to talk about this concept of an 'inner shift in perspective', which is addressed in more detail in the exercises below, but what is important to note is that Kahneman's System 1 (fast, automatic, and unconscious) can be re-programmed, or better conditioned over time through conscious training.

---

10 Vision and breathing are the quickest and most obvious ways to exercise control over an autonomic stimulus. The way we breathe in particular, has a strong effect on how stressed we are feeling. For example, breathing out more slowly will already have a positive effect.

11 A trigger is anything that helps you recall a traumatic memory from the past and bring it to the surface. It can be a word, a smell, a tone of voice, a face, a person, a behaviour, or a situation that makes you feel insecure or anxious. In this way, a trigger is a reminder of a previous overwhelming situation and is an invitation to understand and integrate what lies beneath it.

Conclusion

- We all have two different thought systems: **System 1**, which is fast, continuously active and **unconscious**, and **System 2**, which is slow, only occasionally active and **conscious**.
- Certain circumstances, including **external pressure, can prevent the two systems from working together properly**, and this often leads to an emotional over-reaction.
- We all have our own, unique way in which we evaluate external stimuli, including stress stimuli. The way we deal with **stress is something that we have learned**, so, this means **we can also learn to re-condition it.**

Exercises to go a bit deeper:

This link or QR code will take you to some exercises that will help you become more aware of your red buttons, or stress factors.

→ **www.zen-stories.com/en/zen-e**

Chapter 3

Values and beliefs

The dog in the mirror

Once, in India, there was a little dog running around. He came to a palace and found himself in a room completely lined with mirrors. Suddenly, he saw himself surrounded by a multitude of strange dogs. He thought they were challenging him, so he became angry and started to bark. They all barked back, which made him even angrier. Because none of the 'strange' dogs showed any sign of backing down, the little dog carried on barking and barking until, completely exhausted, he fell down dead.

Years later, another dog found her way into the mirror room. This dog was overwhelmed by the huge number of playmates she saw and started to wag her tail. To her delight, the 'strange' dogs also wagged their tails with pleasure. The dog went on her way, all the richer for this joyful experience.

Questions to reflect on

› *Why did the two dogs react differently?*

› *If the world is a mirror, what underlying emotion does it reflect for you?*

› *How can you tell if something you believe is wrong?*

› *Where is the focus of your attention?*

› *How would you describe your basic attitude to or image of humanity?*

Why did the two dogs react differently?

Their reactions were different because of the way they had been socialised. The first dog had learned that other dogs are untrustworthy and regarded them as enemies, whilst the second dog had a world view based on the existence of trusting relationships.

If the world is a mirror, what underlying emotion does it reflect for you?

If you can name an underlying emotion, that means you already have a fine-grained awareness of your inner processes, but many people are unfamiliar with being aware of their own feelings to this extent. And yet, 'feeling nothing' is also an emotional state or a condition that requires energy. With the help of the limbic system, our brain assigns emotional meaning to events and situations. Through our socialisation and personal experiences, we then internalise these associations unknowingly, but with time and practice we can start to 'see' our emotions again and to do so in a more nuanced way.

How can you tell if something you believe is wrong?

You can do so through critical reflection upon your own behaviour, reactions and the underlying beliefs and values that led to them, as well as through feedback from others. This may seem obvious on one level, but putting it into practice is difficult because of the cognitive distortions arising from System 1 thought patterns. These include 'confirmation bias', which is the tendency to identify, filter and interpret information in a way that confirms our own expectations, and the 'status quo bias', consisting of the inclination to accept the current situation as the baseline reference, and view it as the most desirable state of affairs. Change is subsequently associated with negative emotions and is experienced as loss.

Where is the focus of your attention?

Our attention is often conditioned, habitually and culturally. Is it my fear that drives my focus or my creativity? My (unconscious) fears and the associated avoidance strategies contain great potential. Fears are not bad *per se* – some our natural ones, e.g., the fear of the sabre-toothed tiger ensured our survival – but today many of our fears are social or related to self-esteem. Becoming more aware of them is the first step.

'Your beliefs can be a prison system created by your mind for yourself. But the door is not locked. If you are aware, you can always come out of that.'

Amit Ray

The way we *perceive* ourselves and our environment is, in the first instance, based on our physiological and cognitive characteristics and on our conditioning. The way we behave in response to what we perceive is influenced by several factors, including our personal stress triggers that are established during childhood. Once we become aware of how we respond to pressure, the next step is to transform the way we experience the situation, and therefore the way we behave and respond. To this end, we have to aspire towards genuine, lasting transformation, and this requires us to look inside ourselves first. *All outside change starts with change on the inside.* This is where we hold our beliefs, values and our habitual thought patterns, which ultimately determine our behaviour. To put it another way, psychologically our values and beliefs are located upstream to our behaviour. Like a compass, they help us to navigate the world as we see it through our mental landscape. But in most cases, they also take up time, energy and resources, without us even knowing it. This is why the first step is to become aware of our own mindset. Because creating greater clarity around our values and beliefs is a tried and tested lever for achieving long-term transformation.

During my MBA, I learned about a series of personality tests and leadership inventories that provided me with some helpful insights about myself. But my real breakthrough was in a course exercise that enabled me to discover *my personal values and priorities*. This exercise involved identifying my underlying beliefs, i.e., the rules that led me to feel or experience these values. I discovered that the three things that meant the most to me were recognition, love and learning. For the first time in my life, I was able to observe my own 'operating system', and I subsequently became aware of the many things that lay at the root of my behaviour and my emotions. For example, recognition for me meant my boss, unprompted, noticing that I had achieved something special and praising me for it. By becoming aware of this rule, I was able to change it by balancing 'external praise' more evenly against its opposite, 'self-confidence' – a value that at that time had remained hidden. My new rule was simply this: 'I feel I have gained recognition whenever I remind myself of my previous achievements, successes, or the contributions that I have made.' The solution looked good on paper, but it took me some time to put this rule into practice consistently, and to then benefit from the new experience it brought.

As leaders, it is vital that we are aware of our own values and beliefs, because these constantly influence our decisions and approaches. Once we understand our own values and the priorities they give rise to, we can use them in a constructive way. To do this we need to find a dynamic equilibrium in which individual values are neither distorted nor exaggerated. The model depicted in figure 2 can help us understand this further, but first take a few moments to reflect on the questions below:

› Do you know what your most important values are and what order of priority do they take?
› Do you understand the beliefs that support your values and what it costs you to live by those beliefs?
› Do you know how your personal values are linked to the company values?

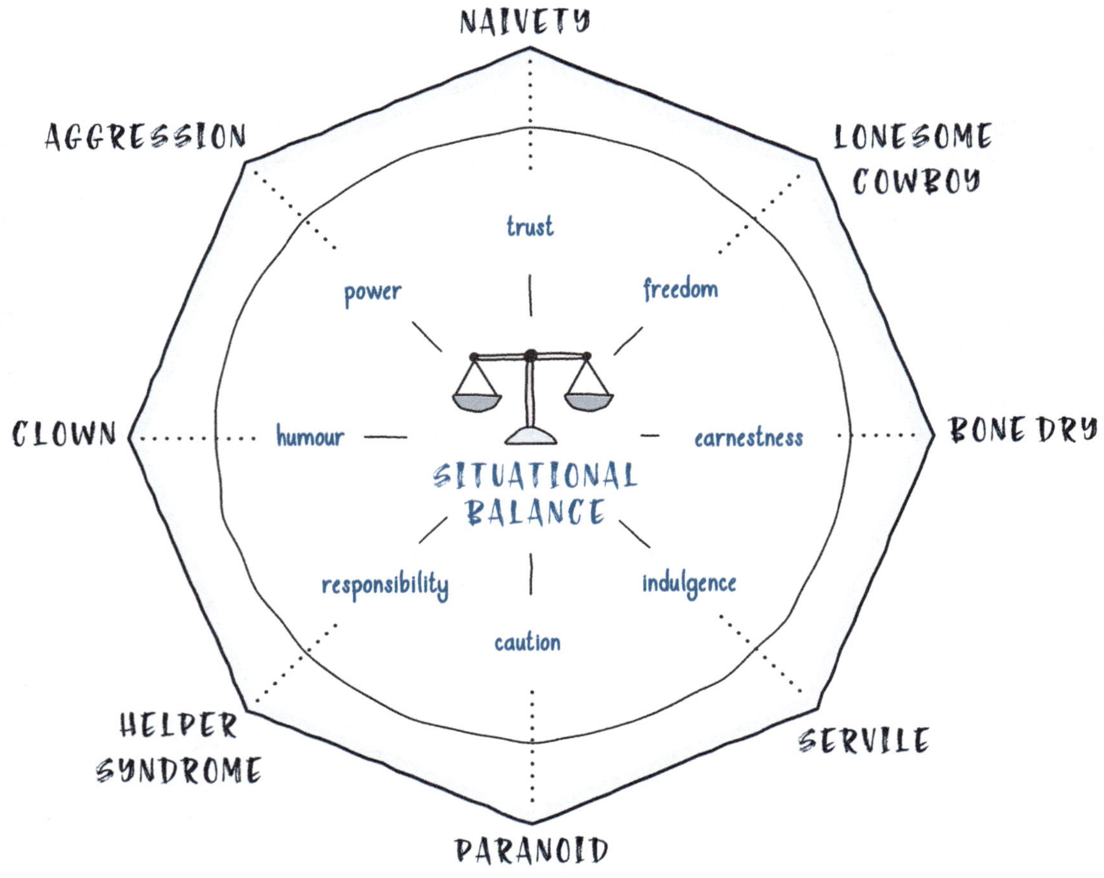

Figure 2: Dynamic equilibrium of values and associated behaviours (based on Bernhard Possert, 2020)

In the dynamic equilibrium model of values and behaviours, all of our values are located on a spectrum in which they are balanced against a counter-value (all of these located within the inner ring). For example, trust is balanced against caution, and humour against earnestness. The right path is always somewhere in the middle, because if we go too far in either direction distortions or imbalances can arise, e.g., where trust tends towards naivety, or excessive caution towards a control mania, or even paranoia in extreme cases. Based on this idea, the values and development square by Schulz von Thun takes things a step further[12]. Each value has an opposite pole, which we can seek to discover, activate and develop. If we have not yet discovered the opposite pole or developed it sufficiently, this leads to undesirable value distortions. Schulz von Thun illustrates this beautifully with the picture of a rainbow – only with the perfect balance of sun and rain does this natural wonder appear in all its colourful splendour.

However, the fact that values have opposite poles is complicated by how, as human beings, we naturally over-emphasise the values that are foremost within our individual personalities. This over-emphasis is due to precisely those beliefs that distort our perception and which could therefore potentially serve as a lever for transformation. It is for this reason that it is worth becoming aware of them and taking a closer look.

What are our beliefs based on? Where do they come from, and what makes them take hold of our minds? Our beliefs do not just come from nowhere, they are the engine that powers our psyche in its drive to satisfy our basic needs. And as well as physical needs, such as eating and getting enough sleep, these also include emotional needs, such as a feeling of security and human closeness, and the quest for recognition and esteem. These beliefs are firmly anchored in the structure of our psyche. They feed on our experiences and our socialisation, gradually evolving into firm, unshakeable assumptions and opinions, enabling us to feel them as certainties that we can hang on to. Having a belief is an established pattern of thought, and an emotional state that usually operates unconsciously.

Beliefs can work on three different dimensions:

› The 'IT' dimension

› The 'WE' dimension

› The 'I' dimension

---

12 In 1989, psychologist and communication expert Friedemann Schulz von Thun added the concept of development to the values square originally created in 1926 by the philosopher Paul Nicolai Hartmann, and thus adapted it for interpersonal communication.

As children, we take it for granted that the Sun 'goes down' in the evening, as this is what our perceptions tell us. Only later do we learn that the Sun is a fixed star, and the Earth revolves around it, spinning on its own axis – so, effectively, it is our own planet that 'goes down'. These facts resonate with the rational part of our psyche, known as the 'IT' dimension. This knowledge may not have much impact on our everyday lives, but despite knowing better, we continue to speak of the 'Sun going down'.

On the other hand, the beliefs we hold about other people, the 'WE' dimension, have a much greater influence on how we see the world, interact with others, and fit into a group. Assumptions such as 'deep down, everyone is good', 'some people are just lazy', or 'XY is the only party you could consider voting for' give us a sense of direction – a compass to navigate our mental landscape – precisely because they are blanket judgements. Blanket judgements are helpful to us in our everyday lives because we do not want to be constantly bogged down with detail and making micro decisions. At the same time, they lead us to fall into old, and therefore unconscious and familiar, thought patterns, which we seldom reflect on or question.

We all have our own peculiarities and for each of our values there is an opposite pole, which we can seek to discover, activate and develop.

It gets even more exciting when we come to the 'I' dimension beliefs because these can lead us to behave in a way that is inappropriate to the given situation. In extreme cases, they can lead us to be 'self-righteous'. Or, going in the other direction, we can be unduly hard on ourselves – we might call this being self-critical or 'self-wrongous'[13]. Either we are convinced of our own infallibility and, by extension, our superiority over others, or we are plagued with self-doubt and the feeling that we are inadequate or incompetent.

This kind of attitude reflects a phenomenon known as 'braking beliefs' and 'accelerator beliefs'. For example, telling ourselves things like 'I'm a clumsy clot' or 'I'm not good enough', 'I've always struggled at learning', rarely helps us to attain a confident, inwardly calm mindset. Instead, telling ourselves things like 'There is a solution to everything', 'I'll get there in the end if I persist', or 'There's a reason for everything, I just need to find it', is more likely to give us a boost.

13 'Self-wrongous' (vs. being 'self-righteous') is a term coined by human behaviour expert John Demartini to point to the polarity that exists within us when it comes to making judgements about ourselves.

This is why it's worth taking a closer look at what puts the brakes on for us. And, unless these braking beliefs evolved from our learning environment, we can generally trace them back to our childhood, just like the stress triggers. The key issues here are having felt unsafe, insecure, or inadequate, or not having been given enough love or recognition – in short, taxing situations in which we, as children, were not felt or seen. In childhood, our psyche is focused on our own existential safety, and situations that jeopardise this can be perceived as a threat. If a relationship breakdown is not acknowledged and co-regulated, this can leave us with a great fear of ever experiencing such a thing again[14]. In turn, this prompts us to try to isolate ourselves from certain past feelings or experiences; sometimes we repress them to the extent that decades later, we still have over-the-top reactions to certain stress triggers (towards our own children, for example), without even being able to understand where the reaction really comes from. The beliefs that arose at the time were a protective mechanism which we used to avoid exposing ourselves to situations we had experienced in the past, as negative or threatening. A belief that has evolved in this way prevents us from stepping back and seeing the full picture. Instead, it leads us to see only a distorted fragment, a partial view. If an issue is charged with emotions that are founded in our childhood, this clouds our perceptions, which in turn restricts the options that are available to us in that moment.

Consciously questioning and reflecting on our own values and beliefs and those of our team and organisation can help us to recognise, resolve or re-interpret beliefs that are 'outdated' or obstructive. This expands our range of options because it enables us to perceive a situation from several additional, new and helpful perspectives. This can resolve the distortion in our values and restore their balance. Only then are we able to draw on our values with good effect and behave more appropriately in the given situation. If we apply the beliefs inside us in a way that is constructive both for ourselves and our employees, we are able to establish on the collective level a values-based culture that is conducive to promoting the desired strategy.

14 In psychology, co-regulation is defined as the way in which the autonomic nervous systems of two individuals interact on the sensory level to enable better emotional balance and physical health.

Conclusion

- Besides our physiology and our stress triggers, **there are also other factors that influence our perceptions and behaviour.**
- **Values and beliefs**, and the priorities we derive from them, are anchored firmly in our psychological structure, **upstream from our behaviour.**
- It is **vital** to become **aware of our own values and beliefs.**
- Each of **our values can only be fully effective if it is in a dynamic equilibrium** with another value.

Exercises to go a bit deeper:

This link or QR code will take you to some exercises that will help you discover your core beliefs and gain a clearer understanding of your values and priorities.

Values and beliefs exercise

→ **www.zen-stories.com/en/zen-e**

Chapter 4

Identity

The sheep-lion

Once upon a time, there was a pregnant she-lion who attacked a flock of sheep. In doing so, she hurt herself badly, so badly that although she managed to give birth to her cub, she herself died. The helpless, vulnerable and confused lion cub aroused the sympathy of one of the mother sheep, who had just lost her lamb. So, the mother sheep took in the lion cub as her own and brought it up with the rest of the flock. It learned to eat like a sheep, to bleat like a sheep, and to run away when danger threatened. It grew up just like a sheep, albeit an inferior one because the other sheep noticed that the 'sheep-lion' was different, and often teased and played tricks on him. And so, the sheep-lion grew to be a shy, unhappy sheep.

One evening the lion king came down from the mountains. When the sheep got wind of him, they bleated with fear and rushed around in a blind panic. The mountain lion sprang and landed right in the middle of them, causing them to scatter in terror. But he was only after the sheep-lion and had no interest in the other sheep at all. He quickly caught up with the sheep-lion, grabbed him by the neck and gave him a good shake. The sheep-lion was paralysed with fear.

'What are you doing here?' growled the mountain lion.

'Meh, meh, I'm just a little sheep. Please don't hurt me, let me go to my mother. Meh, meh,' replied the sheep-lion.

'What's all this nonsense?' asked the lion. 'Where is your mother?'

'There she is, running with the rest of the flock,' replied the sheep-lion. 'Meh, meh, please let me go.'

'But what are you doing here with these sheep?' asked the lion. 'You, the king of all the animals?'

'Meh, meh, I'm afraid,' said the sheep-lion.

'Stop bleating like a sheep!' said the lion. 'You're not a sheep. You are a lion, just like me.'

'No, I'm not,' said the sheep-lion. 'I'm only a poor little sheep, please let me go to my mother.'

'The lion growled, 'Now stop this nonsense, once and for all. You are a lion!'

'Ok, ok,' replied the sheep-lion, 'Maybe I am, but please let me go to my mother.'

At this, the lion grabbed the sheep-lion once again by the scruff of his neck, carried him over to a nearby lake, and held him over the water.

'Look,' he said, 'what do you see?'

'Meh, meh, I can't see anything,' said the sheep-lion.

'Meh, meh, meh! Open your eyes!' ordered the lion.

'I still can't see anything,' replied the sheep-lion.

'Stop panting,' said the lion, 'You're making waves, that's why you can't see anything. Breathe slowly, in and out... That's better. Now, what do you see?'

'I... I... I can see two of you!' stammered the sheep-lion.

'Move your head from side to side,' commanded the lion. 'Now do it again. What do you see?'

The sheep replied, 'One of the lions moves, the other one doesn't!'

'And what does that tell you?' asked the lion.

The young sheep-lion took a good look at the big mountain lion, then looked in the water again. Then he moved once more, put his head on one side, lifted his paw, and looked at the mountain lion again. Now he also noticed that the other reflection in the water was bigger than his one. And, although at first he could hardly believe it, a realisation slowly dawned on the shy, fearful little sheep-lion who was used to being pushed around by all other sheep, 'I am a lion. I am free. I am strong.' He started to roar. Initially it was a timid roar, but it grew steadily louder and more confident. From that time on, he never bleated like a sheep again, but always roared like a lion.

Questions to reflect on

- *Why had the young lion assumed the identity of a sheep?*
- *What was it that enabled him to transform his identity?*
- *What are the key aspects of your identity and what expectations are placed on you?*
- *Whose expectations do you try to live up to? Your own or those of others?*
- *Which parts of your story and the way you tell it are no longer helpful?*
- *Do you generally start your sentences with 'I have to...' or 'I want to...'?*
- *How much of what you did today was simply due to inertia?*
- *Who is your biggest fan and when did you last thank them?*

Why had the young lion assumed the identity of a sheep?

The young lion had foregone his individuality and personal potential in order to fulfil his basic need for security and belonging. Because this attitude was formed unconsciously at an early age, it is difficult for him now to reflect on it and change it.

What was it that enabled him to transform his identity?

It was the feedback and insistence of the mountain lion which brought the young lion to directly experience the contradiction between his long-held beliefs and his physical reality.

Stories help us to make sense of what we have experienced and allow us to connect better with other people. They allow us to understand who we used to be, who we are now, and who we would like to become. Our memories themselves are stories and right from childhood we have listened to stories – not only our own, but also those of others, with fascination. The less helpful elements of our stories give us a set of answers that represented the most meaningful response, according to our world view at the time that the answer was given. Accordingly, a story is not so helpful when used to determine our behaviour in a fixed way. Stories such as these gain their power from repetition and suppress freedom and movement, discouraging openness towards new things. We always have the freedom to reinterpret our stories and to re-tell them in a manner that is supportive and energising for ourselves and others. **Which parts of your story and the way you tell it are no longer helpful?**

Do you generally start your sentences with 'I have to...' or 'I want to...'?

The first phrase, 'I have to...', implies the existence of some (unconscious) authority that determines how things have to be. In this chapter, we will discuss the role and effect of language in the context of personal identity in more detail.

We learn most when we are in a trusting relationship with someone who shows us esteem and good will, or who plays a significant role in our development. Gratitude is the royal road to happiness, **so who is your biggest fan, and when did you last thank them?**

'It's like everyone tells a story about themselves inside their own head. Always. All the time. That story makes you what you are. We build ourselves out of that story.'

Patrick Rothfuss

In April 2016, the Danish company Momondo, which operates a search engine for flights and holiday travel, launched an unusual advertising campaign. Momondo invited people to do a DNA analysis, enticing users by offering as first prize a trip to all the countries featured in their genetic origin. Soon, videos of participants opening their test results were going viral on YouTube. One of those participants was Ellaha, a young woman from Kurdistan in Iran. Ellaha came with her family to Denmark as a refugee when she was six years old, and she explains in her video that she identifies very strongly with her Kurdish culture and history. She is deeply moved by the suffering that the Kurdish people have endured. In her first interview, Ellaha reveals that a part of her has not forgiven the actions of the Turkish government, and that if her DNA analysis revealed she had any Turkish blood herself, she would find this very hard. Despite this, she believes that all people are equal.

Two weeks later she received her test result and opened the envelope with great trepidation – her DNA analysis showed that she is 79% Iranian-Turkish, with some Jewish and European elements. Her initial reaction is one of surprise, but in the end this result allowed her to reconcile and maintain her belief that she is Kurdish, and that she shares a connection with all other human beings, especially those with similar (genetic) origins to her.

The question of identity has fascinated people since ancient times, hence the famous inscription at the Temple of Apollo in Delphi, *'gnôthi seautón'*, which means 'know thyself'[15]. In fact, the oldest koan[16] simply asks 'who am I?' because as a student of Zen Buddhism, learning to know oneself is the sole aim of all endeavours. Meditation is a tool that can help with this, even though what we learn about

15 Interestingly, just below 'gnôthi seautón' is another inscription, 'medèn ágan', which means 'nothing in excess'. This links well with the need that each of our values can only be fully effective if it is in a dynamic equilibrium with another value, i.e., not being expressed in excess (see Chapter 3: Values and beliefs).

16 Koans are key questions or aphorisms of the Zen masters and are used to focus the mind on the contradictory realities and dilemmas of life (see Chapter 6: Polarities). Only a mind of a higher order can escape the pure logic of the words.

ourselves during meditation cannot be captured in words. The fleeting thoughts that come to us give us some sense of how they can captivate us and also limit us. As Zen master Shunryu Suzuki[17] put it, *'Leave your front door and your back door open. Let your thoughts come and go. Just don't serve them tea.'*

The discipline of Western psychology provides us with a more scientific definition of the concept of identity. Who we are depends on the conditions that need to be met in order for our perception of ourselves to remain the same, even when our circumstances change.

As individuals, we seldom reflect on our own psychological identity or perceive it in an objective manner. Heiner Keupp describes the phenomenon of a person, whether us or someone else, as 'an act of social construction', something that is captured in a network of meanings[18]. In this sense, he juxtaposes two questions: 'Who am I?' is set against 'Who am I as the image of myself that I present to my social environment?' To answer these questions, we need to align our subjective 'inner self' with our social 'outer self'. In other words, we reconcile the image we have of ourselves with our place in the social order.

Keupp also uses the term 'social localisation' to describe where we, as individuals, are placed in relation to other people. The fact that it is so important to us to know our place is indicative of our basic human need for acknowledgement and belonging. The act of constantly comparing ourselves with others or looking to see how well we fit into a certain group (be it a group of colleagues or friends, a sports team or a class) takes place almost exclusively on the unconscious level and depending on our personality type, results either in self-affirmation or in confirmation of our own seeming inadequacy.

Swiss psychiatrist Manfred Bleuler expresses this succinctly, *'The important thing in life is to harmonise our varied, often contradictory inner strivings so that despite the contradictions, we can become and remain an 'I', a whole person. At the same time, we have to come to terms with the fact that the external circumstances of our lives never fully correspond to our inner needs, which means we have to adapt ourselves to the reality of our environment.'*

17 Shunryu Suzuki was one of the youngest Zen masters of his era. He helped popularise Zen Buddhism in the USA, where he founded the first Zen monastery outside of Asia.

18 Heiner Keupp, 2020, Essay for Lexikon der Psychologie at www.spektrum.de

Figure 3:
Three forms of identity illustrated through football

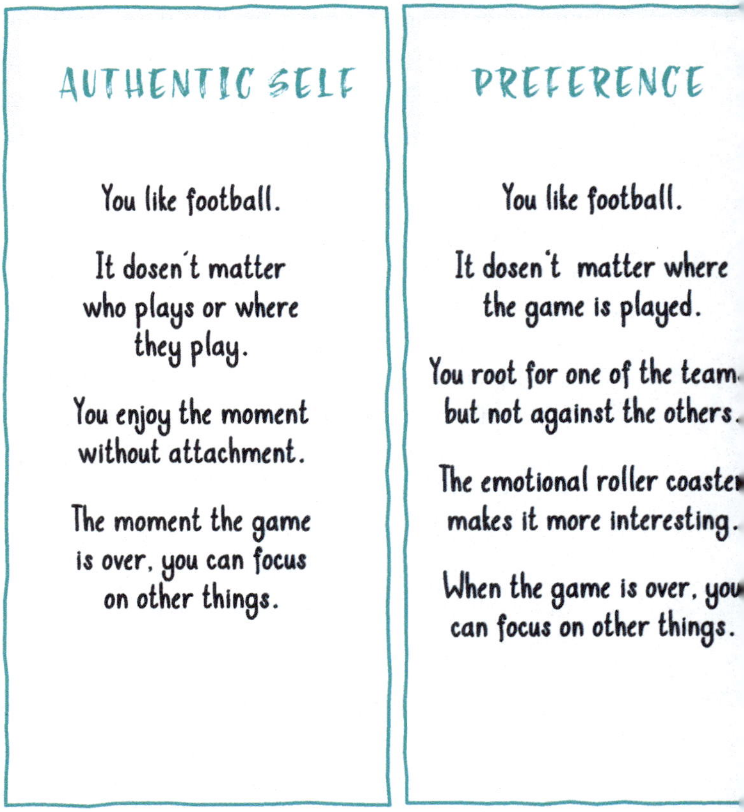

AUTHENTIC SELF

You like football.

It dosen´t matter who plays or where they play.

You enjoy the moment without attachment.

The moment the game is over, you can focus on other things.

PREFERENCE

You like football.

It dosen't matter where the game is played.

You root for one of the team but not against the others.

The emotional roller coaste makes it more interesting.

When the game is over, you can focus on other things.

Aligning what we consider to be our 'self' with the persona that we present outwardly in order to be socially accepted is of huge significance for our mental health, as seen in the cases where we fail to achieve this. According to Bleuler, psychosis can even be the result of an extreme failure in this kind of alignment. By seeing the need for us to align our 'self' and our projected persona more closely, we can then determine how much work we need to do on our identities, and this adjustment is one that is subtle, intentional and ongoing.

We tend not to reflect much on our own identity, and reflections of this kind are often overshadowed by the parallel process of 'group identification'. The original, positive driver for this lies in the most fundamental of all human needs, the need to survive – because our chance of survival is much better in a group than alone. However, our inability as humans to see beyond these group identities can lead to the development of pathological character traits, which makes us susceptible to ideologies. Sadly, this has been proven many times over the course of history.

IDENTITY 1: IDENTIFICATION	IDENTITY 2: INTERNALISATION	IDENTITY 3: FANATICISM
You are a committed fan. The team colours strike an emotional chord. The result affects you on an emotional level. You feel elated when your team wins and frustrated when they lose, and this affects your day and interactions.	Your are a committed fan and this affects your life. The story about victory and defeat is now about you. As a fan, you represent your team to the people around you. You will argue with fans of other teams. Whether you like other people depends on whether they support your team.	You worship your team. The opposing team and fans are your enemy. Relationships mean nothing to you unless the other person is also a fan of your team. You are willing to fight and 'kill' for your team. Your life is about your team.

Despite this, in this context, individuality does not mean separation from the group; instead it means awareness of our own existence in relation to our social network.

Football gives us a good example of how identity can be assumed externally. However strongly we might, as a fan, identify with our team, this only affects our own personal experience. No amount of passion is going to change the outcome of the game, or our team's place in the league tables.

Football is simply a metaphor, it could be easily replaced by other concepts that have an identity-forming function, such as religion or politics. In the world of work, however, identity is generally related to performance. If we identify too strongly with our work, this can quickly tip the balance so that our behaviour becomes unhealthy. For example, we might take start to take things too personally, especially criticism or suggestions for improvement. Similarly, if employees do not dare to criticise the CEO's pet project out of fear for their own jobs (and the CEO's over-identification with his), this creates a risky situation for the company.

It is all the more important therefore to recognise our own identity and be aware that it can be influenced. This is the concept of 'self-authorship'. We never arrive at a single, definitive identity; instead, our identities (in the plural) are the means through which we become who we are.

Who we are and what makes us individuals is largely illustrated in language. Our reality is reflected in the way we put our thoughts into words[19]. For example, if we take a sequence of phrases that express a rising semantic intensity such as 'I feel sad', 'I feel depressed', 'I'm a depressive person', and 'I'm in the grip of a depression'. This illustrates an increasing identification with being depressed. It also shows us how, ultimately, this condition is raised to the status of an object.

On the other hand, through a conscious choice of words we can influence our attitude in a positive way – provided that the attitude is authentic. For example, we can tell ourselves 'I have to do this', 'I should do this', 'I could do this', 'I'd like to do this', 'I want to do this', 'I choose to do this', 'I love doing this.' This is how language enables us to act as a creator, while at the same time making us into the thing being created, especially when we use it without reflection[20].

Closely linked to our personal identities are our daily habits and the actions that go with them. Habits are not necessarily bad. On the contrary, they are an important instrument that our brain uses to safely navigate the daily flood of information and provide us with solutions to recurring challenges – a process which is largely unconscious. These routines free up the frontal cortex, ultimately saving space and energy for other things. Our conscious brain (i.e., System 2) is capable of processing a mere 40 bits of information per second, while our unconscious brain processes millions of bits instead. If our conscious brain had to handle everything, even working at full speed all of the time, it would be fried even before the first meeting of our working day. If our habits are 'programmed' to support our brain and not to bombard it with even more information, this can enable us to enjoy a sense of freedom and vitality which would otherwise not be possible. Without good, healthy habits we will be lacking in energy, without good financial habits we will always have money problems, and without good learning habits we will always have the feeling of not being able to keep up (Clear, 2018).

19 For the German philosopher Martin Heidegger, a truth event is also always a language event. Language is the place where our existence takes shape. Therefore, Heidegger calls language 'the house of being'.

20 See Chapter 1 for more on emotional self-regulation in stressful situations. It is important to be able to draw on a more nuanced vocabulary. If, instead of the generalised 'I feel stressed' response, we actually identify and name the feelings as they arise, this helps us to move on. We may tell ourselves instead: 'I feel helpless', 'I'm afraid', 'I feel inadequate,' etc.

However, acting without conscious thought does not mean we operate thoughtlessly. Instead, it is what enables us to work smoothly without too much background noise. Our minds should not be empty, they should be *free*. By taking away the burden of having to think about every unimportant detail, this frees up our minds and enables us to process what we are actually experiencing. With conscious practice we can train ourselves to respond automatically to certain situations, without having to think everything through from scratch. We should, of course, be aware and mindful of our habits. If we spend most of our time on autopilot, reeling off routines while lost elsewhere in thought, we will not just lose hours of our lives – we'll also miss out on the opportunity to develop ourselves.

How do we cultivate this awareness? The answer is through meditation, especially mindfulness meditation. This teaches us to be mindful in every moment of what we are experiencing, what we can see, hear, feel and touch in the moment; to perceive all this for what it is, and to be aware of the space in which it is happening (see exercises in Chapter 1). And interestingly, if we venture further into the Temple of Apollo in Delphi, we will find another inscription, 'eĩnai', which literally means 'being'[21] – bringing us back full-circle, to Zen (as symbolised by the Ensō on the front cover of this book).

---

21 In all three Abrahamic religions, God's name plays an important role. In Judaism it is considered sacrilegious to speak aloud God's name, JHWH, written without vowels in ancient Hebrew. The name JHWH can be understood as a reference to the Hebrew verb 'to be' (haja, howe); accordingly, God's name is synonymous with the essence of being.

Conclusion

- › **Identity**, in the psychological sense, **provides us** with a constant, **unchanging perception** of ourselves as individuals, even when our external circumstances change.
- › **Identity creates alignment between** the subjective '**inner self**' and the social '**outer self**'.
- › **Subjective identification** is overlaid with how we **identify with groups.**
- › **Habits** and associated actions are **closely linked to identity.**
- › **Habits** are reliable, **unconscious routines** which offer us solutions to recurring challenges.
- › One of the **most effective ways to change our habits** is to concentrate on ***who*** **we would like to be.**

Exercises to go a bit deeper:

Go to this link to download an exercise to help you to explore and analyse the elements that form your identity.

Exercise on identity

→ www.zen-stories.com/en/zen-e

Chapter 5

Collective attitudes

Heaven and hell

Once there was a proud Samurai, with a very quick temper, who had formed the habit of mercilessly striking dead any peasant who showed even the tiniest lack of respect. In those days, Samurai warriors were above the law and this kind of behaviour was generally accepted as normal.

One day, the proud Samurai had killed yet another peasant and was just about to wipe the blood from his sword and put it back in its sheath when all of a sudden, he was afflicted by doubt. He started to wonder whether God would approve of his actions, or whether he would be condemned and consigned to hell.

Because he couldn't get this question out of his mind, he went to consult a Zen master named Kanzaki. With impeccable courtesy, the Samurai laid down his razor-sharp sword, bowed low and asked, 'Please, Master, tell me about heaven and hell?'

Master Kanzaki looked at the man and laughed. He kept on laughing, louder and louder, as if the warrior had said something completely absurd. He pointed his finger at the bewildered Samurai, laughed even louder and cried out, 'You empty-headed son of a moron, you dare to ask me, the wise Master Kanzaki, about heaven and hell? Don't waste my time, idiot! You're far too stupid to understand these things!'

The Samurai, sitting before the master, turned bright red. If anyone else had dared to say such a thing to him, he would have struck them dead instantly. But he made a huge effort to control himself. Master Kanzaki wasn't finished yet. He spoke again, more quietly this time, 'It is quite plain that neither you nor your ancestors have ever used your brains to think about anything. Your entire ancestral line consists of fools and good-for-nothings who would never understand something like this!'

At this, the Samurai was gripped by a murderous rage. He sprang to his feet, pulled his sword from its scabbard, and raised it to cut off the Zen master's head. In this moment, Kanzaki pointed his finger at the Samurai and said, quite calmly, 'Now you see the gates of hell open.' The warrior froze. In that instant he was enlightened and understood the nature of hell. Hell is not a place where you get sent after death, it is an inner state. The warrior fell to his knees, laid aside his sword and bowed his head and said, 'Master, you have my infinite gratitude for this teaching. Thank you, thank you.' But the Zen master just smiled, pointed at him again and said, calmly, 'And now you see the gates of heaven open.

Questions to reflect on

› *In your company, what is heaven and what is hell?*

› *What must people in your company absolutely not do, or must not neglect to do, and what actions are rewarded or celebrated? Are there specific behaviours that are 'punished'?*

› *What are the reasons behind this?*

› *Who in your company drains energy from you and who gives you energy?*

› *What do you especially value about your job/company and what do you dislike?*

In your company, what is heaven and what is hell?

When you reflect on this question, you may discover both some things that conflict and also some things that are in harmony with the circumstances in your company and your own system of values, priorities and beliefs. The things that are in harmony probably inspire you to engage with your work. This is an opportunity for you to reflect further on your personal values system in the context of your company.

What must people in your company absolutely not do, or must not neglect to do, and what actions are rewarded or celebrated? Are there specific behaviours that are 'punished'?

This gives an indication of how the company-specific values system is put into operation.

In companies, just like in other groups of people, there are shared experiences, such as the story of how the company was founded and special events that have had a profound influence on the values system and code of conduct derived from it. In addition, the CEO and leadership team have a strong influence in their role as parents of the system. **In your company, what lies behind all this?**

Who in your company drains energy from you and who gives you energy?

This is an invitation to reflect once again on your own triggers and red buttons.

In the context of having a sense of purpose and direction, **what do you especially value about your job/company, and what do you dislike?**

'Reality is that which, when you stop believing in it, doesn't go away.'

Philip K. Dick

At one time, my team was checking the growth strategy of one of our clients, a global pharmaceutical company, for consistency and to see if there was any untapped potential. We were surprised to find that they didn't have any presence in Argentina and weren't selling any of their international products in this attractive market. When we asked about this, our questions were dismissed out of hand – it seemed clear to everybody that Argentina was of no interest to the company. But we kept on asking and eventually learned that back in the 1970s, the company had done business with some Argentinian wholesalers that had turned sour and ended in heavy losses. This is what gave rise to the corporate belief that Argentina would never even be worth considering.

In their 1996 book *Competing for the Future*, C.K. Prahalad and Gary Hamel alluded to an experiment which illustrated how obstructive, collective attitudes come to be formed[22]. A group of monkeys sit in a cage and stare at a bunch of bananas hanging high above their heads. The bananas can only be reached by climbing a flight of steps. Every time a monkey tries to climb the steps to get the bananas, both it and the rest of the group are sprayed with a strong jet of cold water. In the end, after many failed attempts, the monkeys give up. The zookeeper then removes the hose and changes one of the monkeys for a new one. As expected, as soon as this new monkey sees the bananas, it tries to climb the steps but is quickly stopped by the other monkeys. The new monkey looks confused and keeps on trying to climb the steps, but each time it is held back by the others. In the end, the new monkey accepts the group's code of behaviour and leaves the bananas alone. Over the next week, the zookeeper gradually replaces all the original monkeys in the group with new monkeys who have never experienced the cold-water treatment. What happens? Each new arrival is prevented from climbing the steps by the rest of the group and in the end they all give up. They have internalised the unwritten rule, 'Don't touch the bananas'.

The social fabric of a group often contains strong, albeit unconscious, collective beliefs. Beliefs of this kind often stand in the way of all efforts to promote change.

22 This is more a management fable than an actual experiment that was carried out.

This story illustrates how the social fabric of a group often contains strong, albeit unconscious, collective beliefs. Beliefs of this kind stand in the way of all efforts to promote change, which is why they should be addressed as part of the change process[23]. 'Whatever we do, we mustn't make any mistakes,' or 'We need to excel in all areas' – these are beliefs that can have a counterproductive effect on the attributes that are necessary for change, such as agility, rapid prototyping and ongoing innovation.

The origins of these kinds of beliefs can often be found in collective trauma. Groups of any size, up to and including the whole of society, can undergo psychological experiences of such severity that they trigger a particular response in every member of the group (Hübl 2020). This often gives rise to changes in culture and behaviour. Events such as mass redundancies, the closure of a plant or the failure of a large-scale project can also constitute a traumatic experience, both for the people directly and indirectly involved. For any group, the experience of surviving a traumatic experience together is an important factor in forging a group identity. New members who don't share this collective experience tend to be less integrated in the group, because they are unconsciously branded as outsiders.

At the start of any change process, it is necessary to shed light on the attitudes and beliefs that are specific to your company – first to collectively become aware of them, in order to then examine and question them. Part of this process also involves acknowledging and paying due respect to the stress and emotional burden caused to the team by what they have experienced. This is the only way to process collective trauma and help employees move forward and establish new values that are better suited to a disruptive, creative mindset. Additionally, during the change process, it is important to be proactive in considering the psychological aspects of each change. Ideally, the process design should include targeted opportunities for employees to process their psychological experiences, or else follow-up support should be offered.

23 It takes courage to confront both individual and collective beliefs. In the word 'courage', we can still recognise the Latin root '*cor*', meaning 'heart'. Courage is the emotional fuel for every transformation, and encouraging our employees is an important aspect of leadership.

Conclusion

- **People** in organisations often **have strong, unconscious collective beliefs** that are a hindrance to change management.
- It is important to **make everyone aware** of these company-specific collective attitudes.
- **A transformation process involves examining, questioning and addressing unconscious collective fears.**
  The next step is to **develop new values** that support your company's vision and strategy.

Chapter 6

Polarities

The farmer and the horse

An elderly farmer had only one son to help run the whole farm. They both worked hard and made just enough for a modest living. One day, they were standing out in the field when they saw a magnificent, wild stallion. Surprisingly, the stallion wasn't too shy and after a short while they managed to catch it.

Over the following weeks and months, the son managed to tame the horse, and it proved to be of great help with the farm work. Neighbours came from the surrounding farms to admire the proud animal and congratulated the father and son on their luck. But the farmer answered, 'Is it good luck? Or is it bad luck? Who can tell?' The neighbouring farmers were surprised and went away again.

A few weeks later, during a stormy night, the stallion got out and disappeared into the wilderness. The neighbours came to offer their sympathy to the father and son, though not without a certain schadenfreude. But again, the father said, 'Is it bad luck? Or is it good luck? Who can tell?'

The next day, the son went out to find the stallion and bring it back. After searching for weeks, he came across the stallion in the company of a whole herd of noble horses that had gathered around it in the wilderness. Again, the neighbours were full of envy and praised the fine horses, but the father said, 'Is it good luck? Or is it bad luck? Who can tell?'

With all these horses on the farm, the son soon learned to ride and became a skilled horseman. One day when he was out riding, the horse got panicked by a snake. It threw him off and he was badly injured. The son was no longer able to work on the farm, and his father had to take care of everything by himself. The neighbours all expressed their sympathy, but he replied, 'Is it bad luck? Or is it good luck? Who can tell?'

A few days later, the emperor's army came and rounded up all of the young men in the area, and they had to go and fight in a pointless war against the barbarians. All except for the farmer's son, who was no good as a soldier because of his injuries. This time none of the neighbours came to comment, they were all busy bewailing the loss of their own sons. But the farmer thought to himself, 'Is it good luck? Or is it bad luck? Who can tell?'

Questions to reflect on

› *What is the price you have paid for being too quick to judge a person or a situation?*

› *In this story about the farmer, what changes and what remains the same?*

› *Can you think of any situations in your life that took on quite a different meaning after some time had passed?*

› *What crises have you experienced in your life that helped make you into the person you are, and why did they have this effect?*

When we lived in a primitive societal system in which survival was the sole focus, being able to quickly assess people and situations was an existential skill. Being aware of this evaluation process and being able to question it critically or expand on it is an ability described by the Austrian-born British philosopher Sir Karl Popper in his 'falsification theory'. In practice, this allows us to loosen our unconscious conditioning and make it more flexible. From a survival point of view, there is a clear advantage in System 1-type thinking (see Chapter 1) which enables us to quickly distinguish between friends and enemies – but this comes at the cost of perpetuating our unconscious prejudices. **What is the price you have paid for being too quick to judge a person or a situation?**

In this story about the farmer, what changes and what remains the same? Challenges and turns of fate can only be evaluated with reference to their specific context. Because we are never in command of all the information, it is wise to keep our minds open to other possible meanings, just as the farmer reflects in this story. This story also refers to other concepts, such as 'everything changes and nothing remains still', or the concept of duality: good and bad, positive and negative, cold and hot, dark and light, good luck and bad luck, sadness and happiness. In each instance of duality, an element is held up against its opposite and together they show that in the world we live in, opposite forces can be complementary – they are bound together and dependent on each other.

In the midst of a crisis, we often experience the situation as a kind of punishment. Once we have gained some distance, we can also see it as an opportunity to learn something new, perhaps, or to see the world from a different perspective. The Chinese word for 'crisis' (危机) is composed of two characters, one meaning 'danger' and the other meaning 'chance'. **Can you think of any situations in your life that took on quite a different meaning after some time had passed?**

In order to process and integrate our experience of a critical event, it is important to consciously admit and acknowledge our feelings in connection with the situation. Are we telling the story from the perspective of someone who was a 'victim of the circumstance', or from someone who was able to embrace the situation and take part in shaping it? **What crises have you experienced in your life that helped make you into the person you are, and why did they have this effect?**

'The unlike is joined together, and from differences results the most beautiful harmony.'

Heraclitus

We already know that our personal values can only unleash their full potential if we consciously embrace their opposite poles. Whether we're talking about our values or about culture, business or politics – it's clear that our society is more polarised now than it has ever been in recent history. We can see this in world events, and we can feel it in our relationships and communities – in fact, we often struggle with these conflicting issues in our own hearts and minds. What we need is an integrated perspective that doesn't just generate helpful insights and solutions, but also enables us to experience the world as a richer and more diverse place. In the field of developmental psychology, the ability of an individual to adopt this perspective is seen as a measure of having reached a higher level of awareness and development.

Change processes are a good example to explain polarities. Such processes are often seen by those involved as a problem or at least a challenge that must be solved and addressed accordingly. But on a psychological level, could transformation not also simply be a dilemma between two basic poles of human behaviour? On the one hand, we strive for security and stability, while on the other hand, we seek change or want to adapt as well as possible to changing external circumstances[24]. The degree of tension between these two poles, i.e., how much we tend lean to one side or the other, depends in turn on our individual upbringing, experience and personality, as well as on collective cultural attitudes. As a result of these factors, we have an inherent bias in us that makes us more inclined towards favouring stability or inclined more towards change. The important conclusion for us, as the initiators of a change process, is that neither change nor stability are a problem in themselves, but its rather the perceptions of the people involved in the organisational context that play a decisive role[25].

---

24 This brings to mind the growth drivers of childhood, curiosity and fear, which fuel psychological development, as well as the concepts of the 'comfort zone' and the 'learning zone' which were mentioned in Chapter 1.

25 We tend not to critically examine our perceptions, because we simply assume that what we perceive to be true is in fact true. However, in reality, our perceptions represent opinions, rather than a view of the world that holds absolute validity. All too often our perceptions are distorted by our own thought patterns, due to aspects that we have not integrated into our perspective. Something is truthful when the word and the energy are one, i.e., when we succeed in fully integrating all our personal elements into our view of the world.

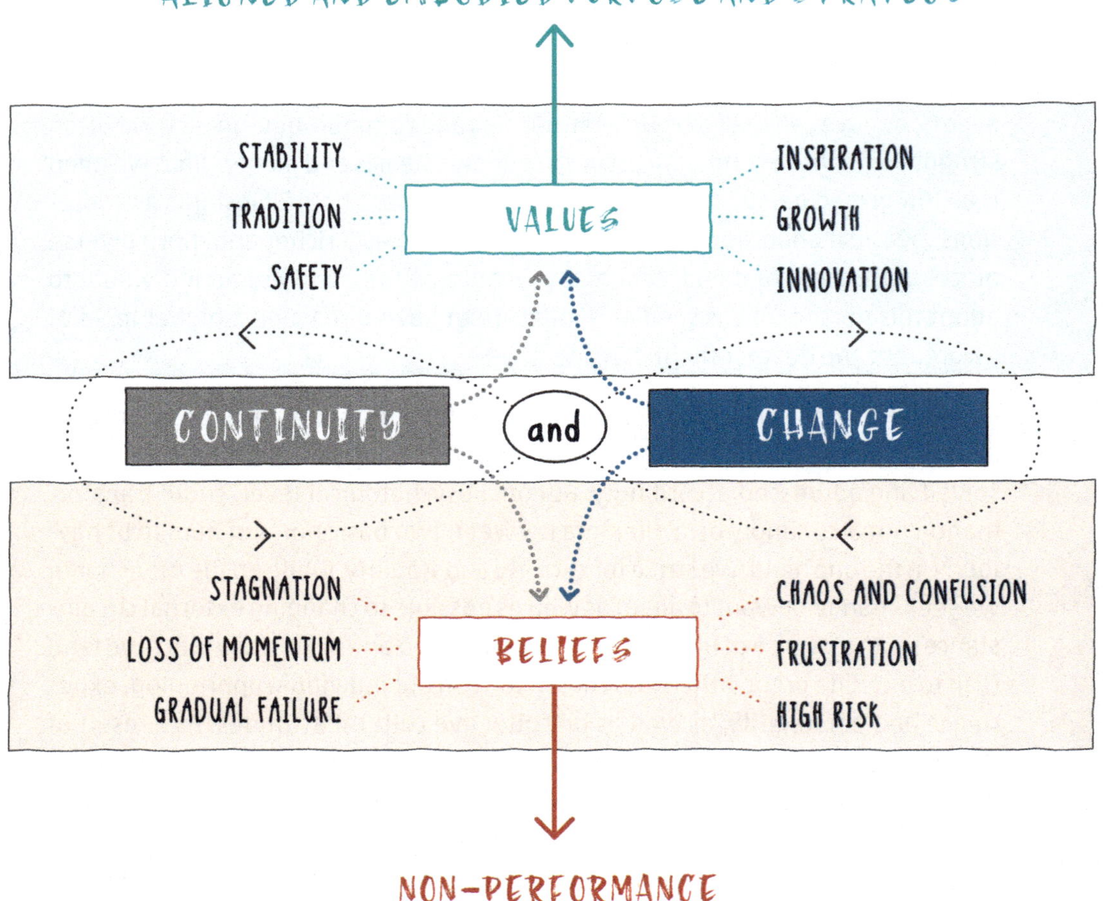

Figure 4: Polarities of values and beliefs in the context of continuity and change (based on Barry Johnson, 2014)

For people who favour continuity, this stands for values like stability, tradition and security. Change, as the opposite pole, then takes on negative associations because it stands instead for uncertainty and stress. For people who favour change over stagnation, it is exactly the other way round – change becomes a source of satisfaction. It also stops our competitors from getting ahead of us, a fear typically held by people of this personality type. Both personality types are pulled towards one pole or the other by their **beliefs**, which are mostly unconscious, and this tendency then gives unconscious support to the internalised positive **values** associated with that pole.

When a company plans to implement a major change process, this is usually based on clear business logic. However, there is usually very little support provided to the employees affected by the change. This is a mistake that can doom the entire process to failure. To avoid this error, it is helpful to first explore and shed light on the fundamental values and limiting beliefs of the people in the organisation.

The managers of successful transformation processes are explicitly aware of the polarity formed between stability and change. Or, to put it more precisely, they are aware of how the employees perceive these two poles. They keep in mind that from this perspective, there is no perfect solution, only a 'best fit' solution. In exploring the topic, they avoid taking an 'either/or' position, and instead try to encourage an inclusive 'this and that' perspective. This kind of sophisticated understanding forms the basis for judiciously aligning all of the employees with the strategic goals. This way, each person is drawn in to engage on the personal level, as well as on the collective level, making it possible to achieve long-term transformation from within, instead of trying to force external, top-down change.

As well as communicating with our employees in advance and keeping them fully informed of the reasons behind the necessary change process and the intended direction, as mentioned earlier, now we can also take our employees' personal needs into account from within the process. A culture of authentic, regular feedback must be included in the design of any transformation process. Being able to see and illustrate the bigger picture is not the only role of a leader; a good leader does not simply drive forward the change end of the polarity, but knows how to draw on and integrate both poles at the right time. If either pole is unbalanced, i.e., overvalued or undervalued, the result will be either chaos or stagnation. Accordingly, the negative pole only comes into play if too much weight has been given to the positive pole. As a leader, it is important to know when to switch between poles. This will enable us to spend as much time as possible in the upper quadrants depicted in figure 4 and minimise our descent to the lower quadrants.

Conclusion

- **Many problems** can be managed successfully if we understand them as **polarities**. In developmental psychology, the ability to adopt an integrated perspective is seen as an indication of having reached a higher level of awareness or development.
- On the psychological level, **change represents a dilemma** between the two **fundamental poles which we as humans strive to attain – stability versus change.**
- From a psychological point of view, it is helpful to see **change** from an inclusive perspective when considering it in connection to stability – **'this *and* that'**, rather than **'either/or'**.
- This sophisticated understanding enables employees, both individually and collectively, to accept both poles and, as a result, forces are aligned, enabling successful translation and implementation of any change process.

Exercises to go a bit deeper:

This exercise will help you to draw up a list of the most important polarities and guide you to explore the unconscious aspects of the poles.

Polarities exercise

→ www.zen-stories.com/en/zen-e

Chapter 7

Living and working with a sense of purpose

The young man and the Zen master

A young man went to see a Zen master. 'Master,' he asked, 'how long will it be until I attain enlightenment?'

'Perhaps ten years,' she replied.

'And what if I make a special effort, how long will it take then?' asked the student.

'In that case it might take twenty years,' replied the Master.

'But I'm willing to endure any hardship,' insisted the young man. 'I want to reach my goal as quickly as possible!'

'In that case,' replied the Master, 'it may take up to forty years!'

Questions to reflect on

- *What does the young man consider to be the best approach to learning and facing challenges?*
- *Which polarity are we dealing with here?*
- *What is the Zen master's message to us?*
- *What are your thoughts on the best way to deal with challenges or reach your learning goals, and what strategies do you use for this?*
- *What are the areas of life where you find that putting in more effort doesn't actually help you achieve your goal?*
- *What do you love doing so much that the words 'success' and 'failure' essentially become irrelevant?*

What does the young man consider to be the best approach to learning and facing challenges?

With total dedication, not sparing any effort, the young man is pursing the goal of 'enlightenment'. But if enlightenment is a form of inner freedom, this begs the question: freedom from what? The young man is focused solely on a goal lying far in the future, a goal he thinks he understands. As a consequence, he completely neglects the dimension of 'being', i.e., awareness of the present moment. And it is precisely this mindset that represents the classic form of conditioning from which the young man seeks to free himself through his pursuit of enlightenment.

Which polarity are we dealing with here?

This is the polarity of 'being' versus 'doing', although in our society the 'being' dimension is generally conceptualised in an abstract way. In contrast, seeing, hearing, smelling, tasting and touching are all direct experiences of 'being'. Every moment of our lives, these channels of experience are filled with perceptions. And even if they're not necessarily dramatic, these perceptions enable us to experience the moment.

What is the Zen master's message to us?

We need to be aware of our own strategies and develop greater awareness of the here and now.

A muscle can only be trained through physical exertion, and after enough time, this effort will yield results. But what emotion do you associate with the word 'effort'? Can you imagine approaching an arduous task with joy and openness? **And what are the areas of life where you find that putting in more effort doesn't actually help you achieve your goal?**

The sheer joy of doing something that is fulfilling, when you are really present and in the 'zone', is for many reward enough. **What do you love doing so much that the words 'success' and 'failure' essentially become irrelevant?**

'He who has a why to live for can bear almost any how.'

Friedrich Nietzsche

The fact that many organisations are not yet giving enough thought to the purpose behind their activities, or to whether their employees share this sense of purpose, is often plain to see in the wording of corporate purpose statements – which still tend to be all about maximising profits. Let's put this into another context – imagine we are going for a drive with some friends, but all that the driver can think about is whether there's enough gas in the tank, how far it is to the next gas station and how to optimise fuel consumption. There's no doubt that this journey would be a much more enriching and meaningful experience for us if, instead of being fully absorbed in the practicalities, the driver took the time to point out the beauty of the landscape, the places of interest along the way, and did their best to make sure that their travelling companions were in good spirits and that their needs were met.

Lips-Wiersma & Wright (2012) showed that when employees feel there is a purpose behind the work they do, this inspires them to engage more with their tasks, leading in turn to increased job satisfaction, stronger motivation, reduced stress and, ultimately, to greater life satisfaction. From this it is clear that having a sense of purpose behind the work we do isn't just something that is 'nice to have'[26] – on the contrary, for most people, having a sense of purpose is such an important psychological need that they would be willing to sacrifice a considerable portion of their income for it. Accordingly, it is in the interests of both employees and employers to create the kind of working environment that answers this need. In nearly all situations, Nietzsche's 'why' from the quote at the start of this chapter could be better replaced by 'to what end', because the answer to this question provides us with a direction, something to aim for, both now and in the future.

When employees feel there is a purpose behind the work they do, this leads to stronger motivation, reduced stress, and to greater work and life satisfaction.

26 Viktor E. Frankl, psychologist and Holocaust survivor, performed research on humankind's existential search for meaning. He coined the expression 'the will to meaning' to describe the primary motivational driving force of all individuals.

Again, it is helpful in this context to look at the inner polarities of the human condition. Here we have two sets of opposite poles: 'self versus others' and 'being versus doing', and a tension that arises between the two. As always, an excessively strong focus on any one of these core human poles creates an imbalance, causing a positive aspect to flip into its negative counterpart. For example, someone who focuses almost exclusively on the dimension of 'being' will radiate authenticity, experience well-being and the acceptance of their fellow human beings; the flipside, however, is that they tend towards inertia when it comes to change, wanting to avoid conflict, which leads to complacency and stagnation. Similarly, a strong emphasis on 'doing' brings the benefits of success, drive, performance and satisfaction, but if taken to the extreme, it can lead to exhaustion and burnout.

What, then, constitutes the polarity of 'self versus others'? The positive aspects of a strong sense of 'self' are independence, freedom and self-expression, but if taken too far, this heads in the direction of egoism and the associated risk of social isolation. If, by contrast, you have a stronger focus on 'others', you are likely to experience connectedness, friendship and social cohesion. But you can have too much of a good thing – taken too far, you may be at risk of exploitation, and you may find yourself imitating your peers instead of being yourself.

A polarity can never be resolved – the two opposing forces are always there. Our aim is not to try and pit one pole against another, but to find a balanced relationship between the two, and to be aware of when too much emphasis on one of the poles threatens to bring negative consequences.

The two pairs of polarities described above have been carefully chosen as an example for this chapter because, in the context of a work environment, they form the four cornerstones of objective judgement. Our presence, our 'being' there, is just as important as the quality of our actions, our performance or the quality of our 'doing', but our needs are also important, especially in the relationship with others. Therefore, it makes sense to combine these four core poles of our humanity into a two-axis model. Each quadrant features the positive attributes that arise when opposing poles are well balanced and reflect the important aspects needed to have a meaningful life, both at work and at home.

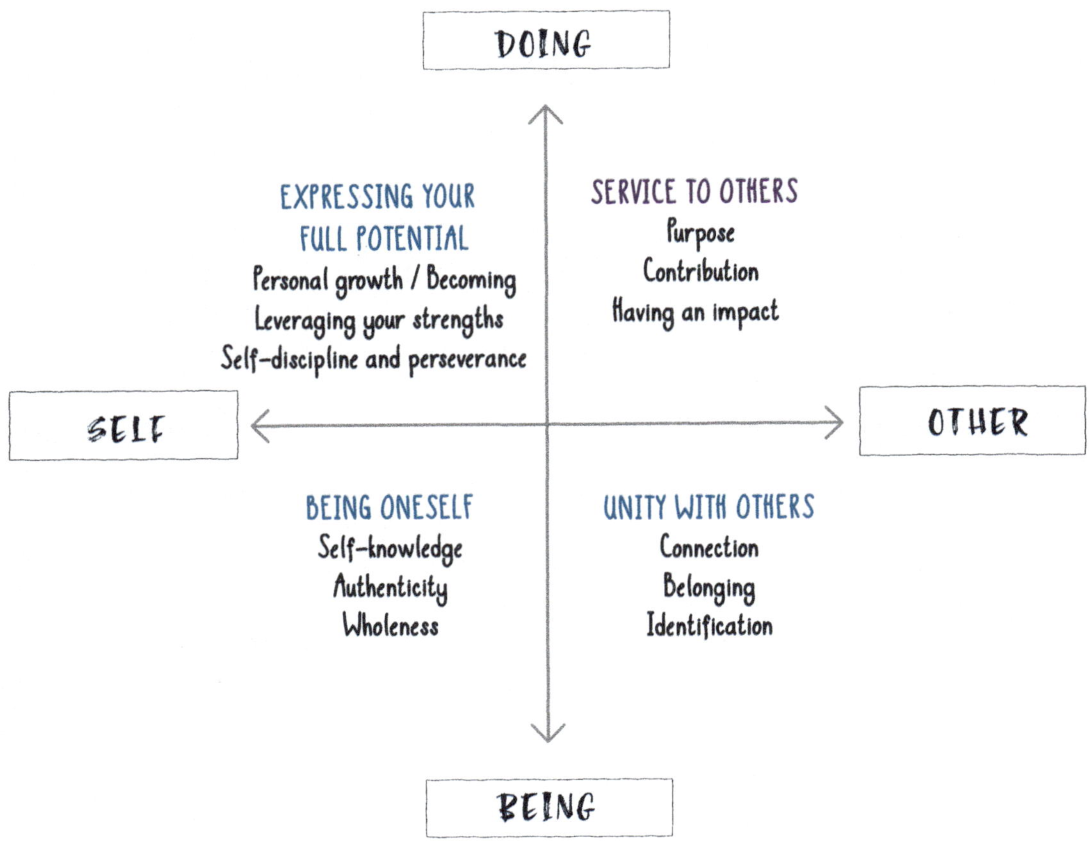

Figure 5: The meaning matrix (based on Lips-Wiersma & Wright, 2012)

› The 'self/being' quadrant helps us to find our ideal state of being. This is the place where we have the space we need to be consciously aware of our thoughts, feelings and experiences. In order to reach this place, we need to achieve a balance between our level of activity and being aware of our own existential being, so that the clarity of our awareness is not blurred by too much busyness. When a person whose brain activity is being monitored with an MRI scanner is instructed to do absolutely nothing, several regions of the brain known as the 'default mode network' will flicker with activity. This type of brain activity reveals, in the first instance, a self-referential trait. When in this state, we primarily think about ourselves and our present situation, in connection with our experiences and conditioning.

- If the same person has been practising meditation or mindfulness for a while and has discovered the silence of their inner space, the MRI scan will show activity in a different region of the cerebral cortex. This region is known as the insula, and it becomes active when we are experiencing the present moment as a collection of all our perceptions arising in the here and now. In this state, we are able to observe our sensations, thoughts and feelings from a distance[27]. This profound experience, which I can highly recommend, turns on its head a philosophical axiom which has profoundly influenced the entire Western world, René Descartes' 'I think, therefore I am', which is transformed into a considerably more natural and relaxed 'I am, therefore I can think'.

- Now let's switch quadrants and focus on 'self/doing'. This is the place where we aspire to realise our full potential, to grow and expand beyond our current state and attain a high degree of personal fulfilment. Important requirements for this are self-discipline, perseverance and focus[28]. Also, we need to be clear about our own values. We need to ask ourselves what is it that interests us most? And what truly inspires and fulfils us in life? On the other end of the spectrum, our aim is to understand what it is that triggers our 'flight, fight or freeze' responses, because these triggers limit us by hindering our ability to think things through and find the best way to respond to a given situation. Gaining these insights makes a huge contribution to our personal growth and to our ability to reach a state of serenity. Seeking targeted feedback from others and using this to calibrate our self-perception and uncover our blind spots is also very helpful.

- The third quadrant represents the relationship between 'being/others' or, in other words, our desire and our ability to connect with the people around us and to develop a greater sense of belonging through things that we have in common. The main point here is the question of our own identity, and by association, how we define inclusion and where we set our personal boundaries. Who I am is also revealed in my boundaries with others as these boundaries protect my sense of self and constitute my autonomy as an individual, but then again, who I am as a person can also be defined in terms of the group or

27 A splendid metaphor illustrating these two systems can be found in the Tora, as well as in Genesis I of the Old Testament. In the Garden of Eden there are two trees, the Tree of Life and the Tree of Knowledge. The Tree of Knowledge allows us to tell good from evil, i.e., to differentiate between the two and to evaluate them - something we mostly do on the unconscious level.

28 Nir Eyal, in his book 'Indistractable', describes how we can keep our attention focused, despite the enormous and often subtle distractions of today's society, including through new technologies.

groups that I belong to. Every attempt to define an identity should be examined to see how consciously it is constructed. And language is important here – whether we choose to describe ourselves in terms of nouns or adjectives has an influence on how we experience life. For example, if we have a preference for adjectives, which are more fluid, involving movement and processes in some way, this indicates that change is in the foreground for us.

› The 'doing/others' quadrant reflects our aspiration to support others and to contribute to the general good of society through our actions. Social commitment provides a direct sense of purpose; it gives us a compass to steer by and creates added value, both for us personally and for society[29].

According to the meaning matrix, the subjective feeling that we are doing meaningful work results from the fulfilment of our personal aspirations in all four quadrants. The positive aspects represented in some of the quadrants will be easier for us to realise while others will require more effort, depending on the main focus of our work and the alignment of our personal needs.

In order to derive specific insights from this matrix, it is helpful to ask the following questions:

› Thinking about your work, which quadrant(s) would you consider to be covered?
› Where can you see possibilities for reaching greater clarity, or what unrealised potential can you identify?
› How would you interpret these quadrants regarding your employees?
› How could you enable your employees to use this conceptual approach to find a sense of purpose in their work?

29 A sense of meaning or purpose comes from congruent somatic, emotional and cognitive expression. When something makes sense, it is true in my body - it feels true, and it is true in my mind.

A meaningful job has several different dimensions which we can categorise. Our aim should be to create enough space for all the different needs and wishes (both our own and those of the team) within the fields of tension spanning the poles and to bring them into harmony. Medical sociologist Aaron Antonovsky coined the phrase 'sense of coherence' to describe this phenomenon. This feeling describes a view of life that is internalised by people who enjoy an especially good state of mental and physical health. It enables them to perceive the world as structured and understandable, to see problems and challenges as surmountable, and to experience their existence and actions as meaningful.

Antonovsky's research in 1997 showed that a feeling of coherence[30] is a predictor for positive health outcomes. It forms the central point of a salutogenesis model[31] in which health is represented not as a condition, not as a mere absence of sickness, but as a field of tension between two poles. Following this school of thought, treating an illness doesn't just mean examining the symptoms and causes; it also involves trying to strengthen the healthy elements that can be found in every person. In this context, the purpose of our existence as human beings and of our work activity, which takes up a large proportion of our lives, is of considerable importance.

30 There are three elements that contribute to a sense of coherence: synchronisation of our cognitive, emotional and somatic elements, alignment with our values and purpose and, finally, harmonisation of our inner and outer world.

31 The term salutogenesis is formed from the Latin word *salus*, which means 'health', and the Greek word *genesis*, which means 'origin'.

Conclusion

- Many organisations **do not put enough emphasis** on **exploring the purpose of their activity and on conveying this sense of purpose to their employees.**
- Feeling that our **work has a purpose** is essential for our psychological **well-being.**
- In this context, it is helpful to look at the **two polarities: 'self versus others'** and **'doing versus being'.**
- By combining the positive aspects of all four poles, we can form **quadrants** representing the areas of tension that span opposing values. These **positive aspects are important in that they enable us to lead a meaningful life, both at work and at home.**

Exercises to go a bit deeper:

This link will take you to some questions about the four quadrants, which can help point you to the areas where you have potential to develop your understanding and gain further insights.

→ **www.zen-stories.com/en/zen-e**

Chapter 8

Harmonising our personal values with the company purpose

The farmer and the corn

Once there was a farmer who grew exceptionally good corn. Every year she won prizes for her crop. One day, a government official was questioning her and discovered that she shared her corn seed with all of her neighbours. The official was surprised. 'How can you afford to share your best corn seed with your competitors?' he asked her.

'Don't you know,' replied the farmer, 'that the wind picks up pollen from the corn plants and blows it from field to field? If my neighbours planted inferior corn, this cross-pollination would affect the quality of my own crops. If I want to grow outstanding corn, I have to help my neighbours grow outstanding corn as well.'

Questions to reflect on

› *What kind of mindset does the official have and why does the farmer's behaviour surprise him?*

› *What is the farmer's attitude towards competition and where does she seek to find it?*

› *What attitude and what message would you take from this story, and how could it apply to your company?*

› *Does your company have a purpose? How inspiring and energising is it?*

What kind of mindset does the official have and why does the farmer's behaviour surprise him?

He can only see the direct competition between the farmers. He is not aware of their inter-dependence, nor of the overarching or interconnected systems that operate together.

What is the farmer's attitude towards competition and where does she seek to find it?

The farmer looks to compete in situations where she can draw on her specific expertise, for example, selecting and cultivating the land, fertilising and taking care of the plants, etc.

What attitude and what message would you take from this story, and how could it apply to your company?

Competition within a company, for example, between departments and roles, is unhelpful and does not represent the best use of company resources. It is instead more constructive to be externally competitive by developing a clear definition of how added value is created for the customer through the differentiating features of a company's products or services, and to align all employees around this.

'What should young people do with their lives today? Many things, obviously. But the most daring thing is to create stable communities in which the terrible disease of loneliness can be cured.'

Kurt Vonnegut

These days most companies have a vision, follow a purpose and make an effort to define the values and behaviours that are desired, by both the company and the employees, to make the vision a reality. These values and behaviours are sometimes known as the 'cultural content' and include a code of conduct, a list of 'dos and don'ts', or other such values-based company 'rules', which can easily be made available to employees. However, 'cultural content' requires the development of 'cultural competence' in order to put these values into practice. Cultural competence needs to be conveyed, learned and internalised as a part of the process of transformation, i.e., it needs to be consciously built into the design of the change programme. This approach enables the participants involved in the transformation process (trainers and team members alike) to discover together what they have in common, forging a bridge which encourages teams to engage actively with the cultural elements of change. This is an important and desired side-effect of the process. A transformation process, by definition, is not a one-off event that can be said to have been completed at a particular point in time; it is instead an ongoing journey, which features regular new departures and developments. Throughout the duration of this journey, the 'momentum of the transformation' needs to be maintained. A successful transformation process needs to reflect all three elements – cultural content, cultural competence and transformation momentum – while also enabling the participants to explore their personal values and priorities.

A successful transformation process needs to reflect all three elements – cultural content, cultural competence and transformation momentum.

The much-quoted axiom 'competition is good for business' is often misunderstood to mean that competition between employees or between company departments is a good thing and should even be encouraged. In the long term, this kind of mindset is unproductive and leads to a culture of mistrust. When we make the shift from merely working alongside each other to truly being together and working with one another, we develop a sense of solidarity, and can then make the conscious decision to align ourselves with our colleagues and form a community with a shared purpose[32].

In order to meet the economic, technological and social challenges arising from disruptive change in a manner which is collaborative, inspired and successful, a company needs to re-orchestrate itself also at the collective level. However, it is individual employees who form the basis of this collective. In Chapter 3, we looked at our personal values, priorities and beliefs. Referring to the concept of mental landscapes, we asked ourselves: Are we aware of our values and are we guided by them? Have we developed our own personal map? The next step is to then consciously determine what is the relationship between our personal values and those of the company or organisation we belong to. The extent to which these two systems are aligned is fundamental when it comes to employee motivation, engagement and commitment. This question is worth considering no matter how long we have been with a company, but especially during times of disruptive change when remaining connected to the company's vision and re-discovering our shared purpose can help change feel less stressful and more worthwhile. This question is really about finding a deeper sense of meaning, discovering areas of fit between our values and those of the company, through the search for an answer. This conscious process helps establish new neuronal connections which can give rise to insights that may enable us to deal with challenges at work in a more open manner, and one which also brings us a greater sense of understanding and fulfilment.

Conclusion

- It is important to distinguish between **cultural content** (values, code of conduct, etc.) and **cultural competence** (the ability to put these values into practice).
- **Transformation is a continuous, consciously designed programme. It is not a one-off event (such as a workshop) but requires a blended mix of integrated elements that are both social and strategically supportive** (e.g., buddy programmes, lunch and learn sessions, team coaching, e-learning, etc.).
- Our personal values give us our own individual **roadmap**. Our task is to **consciously forge a connection between this personal roadmap and the company's purpose.**

32 The shift described here is in fact a change in the focus from 'me' to the other and onto 'we', as we move from the mindset of competing 'against' our colleagues to working 'beside' them, 'with' them and ultimately to supporting and helping them (i.e., we are at the service of our colleagues).

Chapter 9

Inspiring leadership

The Emperor's Cupboard

The emperor of ancient China once ordered a master craftsman to build a cupboard to go in his bedroom in the Imperial Palace. The craftsman, a Zen monk, told the emperor that he wouldn't be able to start the job for five days. The emperor's spies watched the craftsman during this time and saw that he appeared to be just sitting there, doing nothing. Then, after five days had passed, the monk stood up. Within three days he had completed the most extraordinary cupboard anyone had ever seen.

The emperor was extremely pleased but he was also curious, so he had the monk brought to him and asked him what he had been doing for those five days before beginning the work. The monk replied, 'I spent all of the first day emptying my mind of any thoughts of failure or fear of punishment should my work fail to please the emperor. I spent all of the second day emptying my mind of any thoughts that I might be unequal to the task, and any belief that I might lack the skills needed to build a cupboard fit for the emperor. I spent all of the third day letting go of any hope or expectation of obtaining fame, fortune and reward should I succeed in making a cupboard that pleased the emperor. I spent all of the fourth day letting go of any pride that might grow inside me should I succeed in this task and earn praise from the emperor. And I spent all of the fifth day picturing the cupboard clearly in my mind, in the certainty that even an emperor would wish for such a cupboard as you now have before you.'

Questions to reflect on

- *What kind of thoughts most often hold you back from doing amazing things: a) fear of failure, b) self-doubt, c) desire for fame, or d) the expectations of others?*

- *Next time you find yourself thinking like this, how can you identify the initial thought so as to deal with it more constructively?*

- *What parallels do you see between this story and the process you are experiencing while reading this book?*

- *When there is stress or a conflict in a team, what is your behavioural pattern?*

What kind of thoughts most often hold you back from doing amazing things: a) fear of failure, b) self-doubt, c) desire for fame, or d) the expectations of others?

Once again, this is an opportunity for you to reflect on beliefs you hold that 'put the brakes on' in the context of your leadership role.

Next time you find yourself thinking like this, how can you identify the initial thought so as to deal with it more constructively?

Simply being aware that your 'braking' beliefs have just been activated is helpful in itself. Awareness is all it takes to enable you to make better decisions.

What parallels do you see between reading this story and the process you are experiencing while reading this book?

The monk becomes aware of his limiting beliefs that have been activated. By meditating on these beliefs, he is able to gain a sense of distance and is no longer unconsciously held captive by them. Hopefully, as you read this book you are reflecting on each chapter, thereby going through a similar process.

Archetypes of reactive behaviour can point to the important, recurring 'stories' that happen in many teams. Examples of three major reactive archetypes include:

1. Leaning in on the task, being very directive, taking control of the situation, making goal-orientated and quick decisions, assigning roles and delegating tasks.
2. Being concerned about those in the team, sensing what is going on and wanting to please, not wanting to make rushed decisions and concerned with bringing about harmony.
3. Leaning out, as if not being a part of the team, seeing little sense in the team's activities, pretending to be strong and independent, being cynical and using humour to alienate themselves from the team.

No matter how others behave, what is more telling is how they feel about things. And if this feeling is stressful in some way, it is probably a trauma reaction. **When there is stress or a conflict in a team, what is your behavioural pattern?**

'A good leader inspires people to have confidence in the leader; a great leader inspires people to have confidence in themselves.'

Eleanor Roosevelt

With every transformation process, there are many factors that have a bearing on its success, but one of the most important is inspiring leadership. It is for this reason that, in this chapter, we will focus on the essential role a leader or leadership team plays in both understanding the psychological dimensions of change and having the ability to communicate, in a convincing way, the purpose behind the change.

Leaders must lead by example: a leader is expected to act as a clear role model, embodying an inner change in perspective that inevitably accompanies outside change. It is therefore important that the leader shares their personal experience of the change. Part of this narrative should point out the issues that are already clear and have been decided upon and identify those that are yet to be developed in the course of the change process. Not only does this generate a sense of authenticity, but it also gives those involved a chance to engage and to have the freedom to have a hand in shaping their own future. It will come as no surprise that allowing employees a 'space to dream' can increase their commitment to the change. When Martin Luther King gave his famous speech in Washington in 1963, he did not start with 'I have a plan'. Instead, he used the much more inspiring opening 'I have a dream...'.

For a company to be well positioned for the future, it needs a leadership team that can convey a clear and meaningful picture of that future – a vision that inspires everyone involved and invites them to engage with it[33]. And it needs a programme that incorporates both the structural and psychological aspects of transformation in a balanced way. The design of such a programme responds to the specific cultural situation of the employees and must also encourage and empower them to dare to try new things.

---

33 By 'vision' we mean 'a dream with a deadline', or that at least certain aspects of the vision must have a concrete end point. At the end of the day, a vision is a positive fantasy about the future. Accordingly, we can apply the formula courage = vision > fear, as fear represents a negative fantasy about a possible future. It is important that the vision is not purely an intellectual exercise but that it is also grounded in emotions that encourage those involved to strive towards it in their actions. Finding a goal structures our perception, and as soon we aim at something, our brain and the perceptual structures re-orientate themselves to calculate a pathway towards the goal.

Every transformation process has its own ideal tempo. Companies often make the mistake of trying to fast-track the process and are then astonished at the resistance this generates. Resistance to a transformation process develops in proportion to the scale and pace of the change – it cannot be measured in terms of whether the change is perceived as advantageous or not. In the latter case, change is still possible, but can only be sustained for a short period of time.

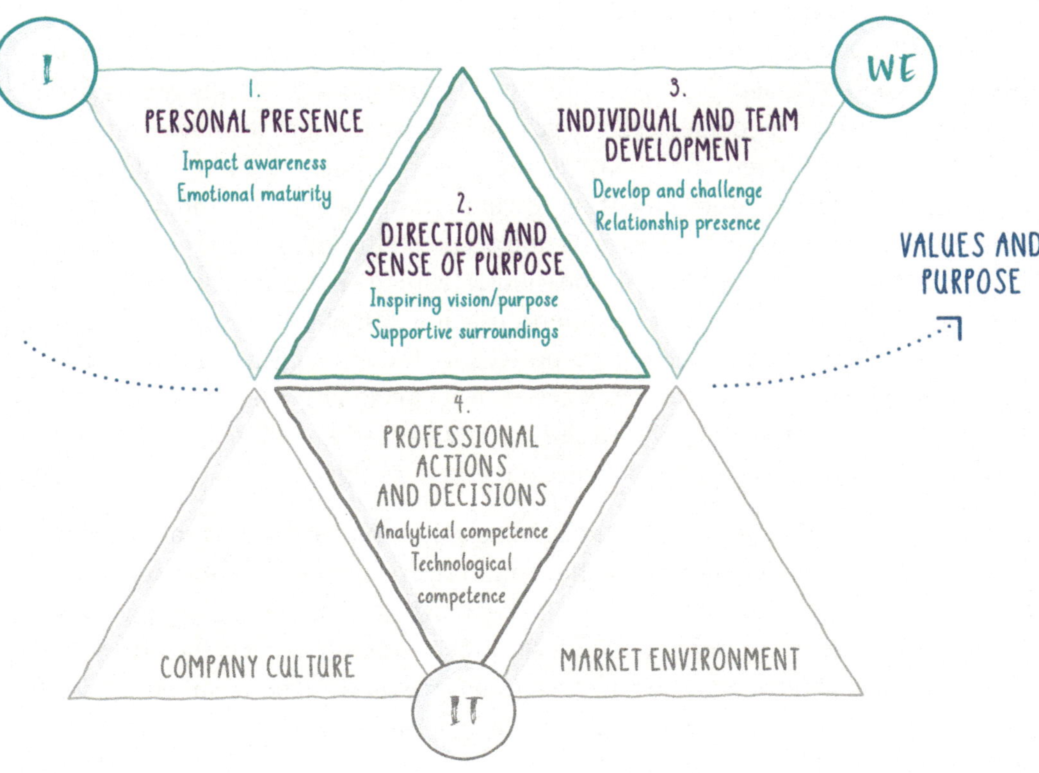

Figure 6: The leadership effectiveness map

As leaders, it is vital for us to know how effective our leadership is and how we can enhance our performance to create even more impact. The leadership effectiveness map in figure 6 represents four dimensions, which incorporate the issues we have discussed so far, interlocked by the three cornerstones of 'I', 'WE' and 'IT'[34]. Leadership quality or effectiveness can be measured by whether those working with a leader are growing and flourishing, both as professionals and as individuals, or whether they are getting left behind. Let's explore how this map can support us as leaders.

The first dimension, **personal presence**, describes the impact that we, as individuals, have on others. This could be either through a higher level of emotional maturity combined with the ability to regulate our own emotions, or through our own integrity with regard to personal values that we have thought through in a conscious and considered way; it could also be through the authenticity we project when we present ourselves. To successfully drive forward the development of a team, a department, or an organisation, we as leaders and the leadership team need to have a good level of self-awareness and an understanding of the impact we have on others. Because we too act under the influence of our socialisation and the patterns we have unconsciously learned – patterns that can lead us 'to think inside the box', or more humorously illustrated by the saying 'I don't know who discovered water, but I'm pretty sure it wasn't a fish!' – because we don't know what we don't know[35]. To enhance our personal presence, we need to come full circle in the process of raising our awareness. Knowing first what our inner drivers are can help us to enhance our external impact.

To change our self-awareness, we need to be able to recognise and regulate our own emotions. This is a recap from the topic of stress triggers covered in Chapter 2. When situations, people or certain behaviours cause us stress, triggering a 'fight, flight or freeze' response, our capacity for decision-making is unconsciously distorted, and we tend to slip automatically into survival mode. In this mode, access to our inner resources is drastically reduced as adrenaline and noradrenaline kick in, limiting our ability to think and act rationally. 'Fight or flight' in the business context does not mean literally fighting or running away, but if, for example, we leave the room before a discussion is properly concluded because we

34 Created by Aergon, in collaboration with Amanda Keller from Leap Consulting.

35 This is the subject of a whole series of development models, e.g., Beck et al. (2005), Cook-Greuter (2010), and Etchery et al. (2013), all of which provide potential for personal assessments.

feel anxious, or if we distance ourselves cognitively and emotionally from others in order to cope, these behaviours could be seen as stress responses. And as stressed leaders, we in turn are more likely to trigger stress responses in our employees (a phenomenon known as emotional contagion). In this kind of environment, characterised by reactive responses, it is very difficult for creativity and constructive collaboration to flourish. Nor does it encourage people to take personal responsibility. If we are aware of the impact that we have on others, and if we understand the mechanisms involved, we are in a stronger position to exert influence. Self-reflection and seeking regular feedback, together with meditation and contemplation exercises, can enhance our awareness of our personal impact and help us to develop greater emotional maturity.

The second dimension on the map is **direction and sense of purpose**. It is helpful in this context to develop an inner compass, to be aware of our values, priorities and our sense of purpose. Incorporating our values into our habits and actions makes them visible, and over time leads to us embodying them. Only then can our *raison d'être* encompass more than just meeting our need for security and satisfying our ego. Only then will we discover a clear, inspiring direction and, beyond that, our sense of purpose in an increasingly complex world.

Adopting a consistent, understandable position lends us authenticity as a leader, which in turn makes our leadership feel tangible to others. This requires that we show ourselves fully, without pretending that our rough edges do not exist. There should be alignment between our thoughts, feelings, words and actions, and we will be seen as being congruent. Being truly authentic, i.e., aligned in the way described above, requires courage, but at the same time, it is also the fuel that drives personal growth.

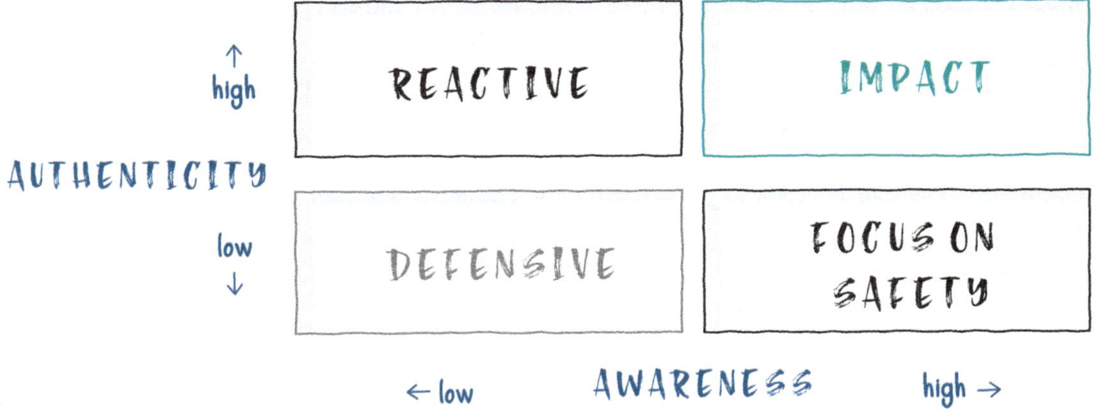

Figure 7: Personal leadership styles

If we take the aspects of self-awareness and awareness of our personal impact together with authenticity, we can create a matrix of leadership styles and their associated behaviours (see figure 7 above)[36].

If we as leaders do not behave with authenticity and do not have much self-awareness or awareness of our personal impact, we tend to act defensively as default. This is because we may lack the courage needed to stand up for our own values and beliefs (authenticity), as well as the ability to reflect on and regulate our emotions (awareness). This results in a leadership style characterised by a survival mode mentality, in which we see any unforeseen event as a threat.

If as leaders, however, we are authentic in our behaviour but still lack self-awareness and awareness of our personal impact, this also causes problems. As long as we are unable to regulate our emotions, we will be susceptible to stress triggers, and will act instinctively and reactively to perceived threats[37]. Similarly, if we are

36 A more nuanced approach is based on action logic, with seven distinct leadership awareness categories, which was developed and quantified by Rooke and Torbert in 2005.

37 The Dunning-Kruger effect is a cognitive distortion in which people think that they are cleverer and more able than they really are. When we find ourselves in an area in which we have very little experience, we also lack the ability to judge our own lack of competence. This combination of under-developed awareness and limited self-reflection can lead us to vastly overestimate our own abilities.

aware of our emotions and responses but lack clear direction, it results in behaviour that is focused primarily on safety, and that smothers any potential growth.

Ideally, as leaders, we should combine authenticity with self-awareness and awareness of our impact, i.e., a high level of emotional intelligence. Only then will we be able to realise our potential and create impact through our presence and our actions.

Recognising our own values and beliefs and aligning them with the company's purpose can help to create a sense of meaning, and can also result in creating added value for the company. But this raises a question: does our role as leaders also encompass forming our own sense of purpose and recognising and developing our personal values? Leadership theories, such as transformational leadership and mindful leadership, answer this with a resounding yes!

The influence of personal presence, the first dimension, on our impact as leaders has been extensively discussed in recent years. Leadership styles such as 'mindful leadership', 'servant leadership' and 'compassionate leadership', as well as questions around integrity and maturity, highlight the importance of reflecting on our emotions and being aware of our personal impact.

As leaders, we are often under the spotlight, and this enhances the impact of our personal presence. When it comes to leadership matters such as authority, loyalty, inspiration and acting as a role model, it is essential to have our own clear values that we have thought through, and that we are willing to consistently stand up for.

Some questions to consider:

› What different levels does leadership work on and what factors influence its effectiveness?
› What are the leadership needs of our employees and of our company?
› How can we, as leaders, meet these needs or at least consciously work towards meeting them?

The third dimension is the **relationship between leaders and employees**. It is worth reflecting on the nature of this relationship in our organisation. Is it authoritarian, directive, or participatory? Is there esteem, support and/or encouragement? To what extent do we consciously develop our relationship with our employees, and where do we set the boundaries? Do we have a clear understanding of their individual needs and abilities? Do we lead, challenge and promote them accordingly? And, of course, there are also relationships between employees, and the totality of these relationships is reflected in a company's culture.

Are there certain behaviours that prompt us to intervene decisively? Are we aware of conflicts between employees? Do we consider it to be part of our role as leaders to influence how employees interact with each other? Over the last few years, under the catchphrase 'the manager as coach', there has been an upswell of support for providing targeted development to individual employees. This model represents a wealth of potential for putting our skills to use in an effective and supportive way. And we can do this through various means, including mindful communication and quality relationship-building.

Now we come to the fourth and final dimension, the **relationship between employees and their work (professional actions and decisions)**, which represents an almost definitive aspect of leadership. Let's ask ourselves: Do we give clear instructions, and do we insist on performance? Do we monitor the results? Do we give our employees support when they need it? The answers to these questions give a pragmatic, operational perspective on how work gets done in the company. All this is summarised under the term 'management', and is clearly focused on the organisational aspect of work. This differs from the concept of 'leadership'. As leaders, our focus is on motivating and inspiring our employees and encouraging them to be self-reliant. Both management and leadership are necessary in order to give our employees direction and a sense of purpose in their work.

Implementing concrete professional measures and decisions is a critical factor in how effective we are as leaders. If we are leading a company in the wrong direction and if our output does not meet the required standards, this will be detrimental both to the company's performance and to our authority as leaders, in the eyes of employees. These days, decisions are often complex and challenging, and it is very hard to assess the probability of their successful implementation. Often, we are simply unable to say with certainty whether or not we are going to achieve the goal we have set ourselves. However, instead of persisting doggedly in the search for the perfect solution, what leaders need is a robust decision-making process – a process which involves genuinely listening to both experts and employees and acting based on the facts, taking into account the corporate objectives – while weighing all of this against the company's values and principles.

Together, these four dimensions form a map of our personal leadership potential. By clearly demonstrating our leadership style and by drawing on a wide repertoire of leadership techniques, we can enhance our personal influence and use it in a constructive way. Otherwise, our potential lies dormant. What's important here is not to try and become the ideal leader, but to develop breadth and depth in our leadership approach.

Conclusion

- For a successful **transformation**, it is essential to gain a **better understanding** of the psychological dimensions of change, to **communicate the purpose behind it** and to **lead from the front, as a role model. Personal presence, awareness of our own impact** and **genuine emotional maturity** are **key elements of inspirational leadership.**
- Combining **authenticity with a high level of self-awareness and awareness of our personal impact** will enable us to act successfully as leaders.

Exercises to go a bit deeper:

This link will take you to external providers who offer personal assessments regarding your level of awareness and preferred approach to complex problems.

→ www.zen-stories.com/en/zen-e

Chapter 10

Empowerment

Archery

A Zen master was watching her students practise archery and noticed one of them who kept missing the target. She said to the student, 'It is your desire to win that saps your strength'.

In Kyūdō, which is the Zen name for an ancient form of archery, one of the central ideas is that by practising a physical activity for many years, it should become effortless, both mentally and physically. This means we can carry out difficult, complex movements without consciously exerting our will, i.e., controlling them with our minds. And in doing so, the archer 'becomes one' with the act (or art) of archery.

In psychology, a mental state in which we experience an exhilarating feeling of being fully immersed and absorbed in an activity is called 'flow'[38].

38 The flow theory, developed by Mihály Csíkszentmihályi (1924-2021), Professor of Psychology at the University of Chicago, explains that people who engage in an intrinsically motivated activity have a characteristic experience. This is the experience described as 'flow' and involves being completely absorbed in the activity.

Questions to reflect on

› *Can you think of moments when you have experienced 'flow' in your work and in your team? What were the ingredients?*

› *How can 'flow' apply to leaders and employees?*

How can 'flow' apply to leaders and employees?

In order for employees to experience flow, the right person needs to be matched with the right task. The match is ideal when the difficulty of the task corresponds well with the employee's abilities but still contains a bit of a challenge. This is when we can expect the greatest level of intrinsic motivation, i.e., the employee is enthusiastic and gets the job done without effort, but it stretches them without it being stressful. When in a state of flow, employees do not just deliver their maximum performance, but rather their peak or optimum performance. What's more, after a flow experience, they are still able to continue to be productive because flow experiences are not exhausting; quite the opposite, in fact. The key to a flow experience is harmonising our inner and outer world (see Chapter 7 where we explored the elements that give rise to a sense of coherence). Having a better understanding of our personal values and priorities, as well as participating in tasks that are tailored to our abilities and talents, can increase the likelihood of a flow experience.

Flow can also be experienced in a team if psychological safety and interpersonal trust are present and if there is an appreciation among team members that they can take social risks such as admitting mistakes or asking for help. To achieve this, leaders must be able to spot the early signs of stress or possible conflict and help resolve them so that trust and psychological safety are maintained. Flow, then, becomes a prerequisite for innovation and growth.

'Leadership is not about control but service. It's not about power but empowerment.'

Myles Munroe

These days, 'empowerment' is something of a buzzword. It means, quite literally, giving someone the power to act on their own behalf. Practically, it means providing the support and resources that employees need to act autonomously. Strengthening and developing an employee's existing abilities makes it possible to give them greater responsibility, which in turn increases their degree of autonomy and self-determination. In recent business history, there have been plenty of examples showing that decentralised, self-organised teams can achieve extraordinary results. This should come as no surprise. Empowering employees leads to better performance, higher satisfaction and more engagement (Lee et al. 2017). However, it is often misunderstood that autonomy alone leads to better results. On the contrary, autonomy without the right conditions can lead to employees feeling overwhelmed, making poor decisions and ultimately being less productive.

To avoid this, it is important to create a working environment that is based on trust. Having to make decisions independently is a challenge that often pushes employees outside their comfort zone. In this context, a culture of psychological safety is vital, as it enables any unresolved issues, doubts or potential difficulties to be discussed in an open and supportive manner, and ensures they are not ignored or suppressed out of fear or shame. And as the carriers of culture, leaders must model and promote the behaviours that create psychological safety. With these elements in place, a connection then needs to be made with the vision and shared purpose of the company. It is essential that everyone is on the same page with regard to the company's vision and the processes and structures that lead to it (strategy). It is also important that everyone is clear on the values and principles that should be reflected in their behaviour. However, to achieve this state of shared alignment between leaders and employees, it is not enough to simply communicate the company's vision, strategy and values system in a clear and understandable manner. Instead, these aspects must be internalised through 'cultural competence' training (as discussed in Chapter 8). To this end, it is helpful to have a shared language and a collective competency model that is applied in practice and serves as a reference framework. In his classic book *Alice in Wonderland,* Lewis Carroll neatly expresses how important it is to have a (common) goal.

When Alice comes across the Cheshire cat in the forest and asks it which way she should go, that cat replies, 'That depends a good deal on where you want to get to'. When Alice responds that she doesn't care much about the destination, the cat says, 'Then it doesn't matter which way you go'.

Of course, as leaders, we need to let go of the reins at some point. Completely. This means giving our employees our trust in advance. It also means relinquishing control and being open to the possibility that the solutions or proposals that emerge may not fully correspond to our own ideas. For leaders who like to keep a firm grasp on details at all times, this can be the most difficult step to take. But unless we do it, empowerment is doomed to fail because empowerment, by its very nature, leads to diversified outcomes. And this diversification is the cradle of innovation. Only when we, as leaders, are willing to engage with new solutions, will empowerment bring successful results for all concerned. It is just as Steve Jobs said, 'It doesn't make sense to hire smart people and tell them what to do. We hire smart people so they can tell us what to do'. It is the duty of every leader to convey trust and provide a sense of direction (the what and the why), while leaving room for creativity (the how) (Bungay, 2011).

It is the duty of every leader to convey trust and provide a sense of direction, while leaving room for creativity.

Each of these two conditions, trust and direction, represent a *conditio sine qua non*, an 'essential prerequisite'. Once they are in place, there is the autonomy to make an informed, uncoerced decision on 'the how', which results in a feeling of empowerment. The field of tension between the two poles of autonomy versus shared alignment gives rise to another interesting matrix.

Figure 8: Degree of alignment and autonomy

In a company where employees have little autonomy and no shared sense of alignment, we often find a hierarchical leadership style which is characterised by micro-management, siloed thinking and unilateral decision-making. If, on the other hand, employees have more autonomy, but do not have a shared sense of alignment, this merely results in a lack of coordinated activity. In addition, greater autonomy increases the level of complexity in the work environment, which often results in added stress for employees[39]. So enhancing autonomy without

39 In order to reduce complexity, the Cynefin framework is a helpful conceptual framework that offers five decision-making contexts or domains – clear, complicated, complex, chaotic and confusion – that can help leaders identify how they perceive situations and make sense of their own and other people's behaviour, in order to support decision-making (Snowden & Boone, 2007). Bill Gates, American entrepreneur and philanthropist, expressed it aptly, 'The barrier to change is not too little caring; it is too much complexity. To turn caring into action, we need to see a problem, see a solution, and see the impact. But complexity blocks all three steps.'

also matching this with alignment will negatively impact on any company's culture and results. When empowerment works properly (i.e., alignment and autonomy are both optimised), it promotes creativity and the emergence of agile, elegant solutions for new challenges.

It also fosters 'organisational citizenship behaviour', a positive behaviour where employees 'go the extra mile' out of personal motivation, and in doing so support their colleagues and benefit the organisation as a whole. Organisational citizenship is neither required nor formally rewarded but is indispensable to the company's success. This kind of behaviour may include, for example, taking care of a task even though it is beyond our remit.

This makes empowerment, when implemented in a conscious and constructive way, an approach that leads to better-performing employees and teams who are more satisfied and more dedicated to their work (and their company).

Conclusion

› The prerequisites for empowerment are a trustful, **psychologically safe, transparent** and **constructive working environment**, where there is clarity with regard to the company's goal and strategy, values are shared and practised, and supportive behavioural principles have been established.

› **Empowerment** leads to added value when the employees and leaders **are aligned with one another** in pursuit of the company's goals and vision and have the freedom, within this framework, to act with a **high degree of autonomy**.

Chapter 11

Starting small: real communication in practice

The enlightened one

Once, there was a monastery deep in the woods that was home to a handful of ageing nuns and monks. The monastery had grown old and decrepit, just like its inhabitants, because over the years only the most urgent repairs had been done. Also, for many years now, no apprentices or novices had joined the community. Each nun and each monk went about their duties on their own, only coming together for meditation and for the weekly meetings in which the tasks were allocated. These meetings were always plagued with disagreements and petty squabbles would frequently flare up between the nuns and monks.

One day, at yet another of these unpleasant meetings, the old abbot could bear it no longer, 'We are nuns and monks and many years ago, we chose a life of seclusion, forsaking the world in order to meditate and find inner peace. Now we're bickering over the most trivial of things. What has happened to us?' The deadly silence that followed this speech weighed heavily upon everyone who heard it, and they all looked at each other in consternation. After a lengthy pause, the abbot spoke again, 'I simply don't know what else to do, so I've decided to visit the old Zen master and consult her about our situation. It will be a long and arduous journey. But I will leave tomorrow at sunrise.' He then stood up and left the room.

After walking for nearly two weeks, he finally arrived at the house of the Zen master. She greeted him warmly, embraced him and invited him in for tea. After they had sat there a while, sipping delicious hot tea without saying a word, the Zen master broke the silence, 'What brings you here to me? We're both getting on in years, and the journey here from the monastery is long and gruelling.'

The abbot needed a few minutes to collect himself. Then he spoke, 'We are always quarrelling with one another, those of us who are left. Things simply can't go on like this for much longer – it will be the end of the monastery. I don't know what to do.'

The Zen master looked at him for a long time, with a warm expression full of empathy. Then she said, 'It's late, and you've just been on a long journey. Go to bed now. I will meditate on your question and give you my answer in the morning.' Feeling relieved, the abbot went to bed and sank into a deep, restful sleep.

The next morning, he sprang out of bed, refreshed and full of energy, and hurried to the Zen master. She was already up and seated at the table, and she handed him a cup of steaming tea, without uttering a word. They sat in silence for a long time, until she said, 'I have meditated on the challenges you and your brother and sister monks are having, and this morning I have been visited by a wonderful insight – one of the inhabitants of your monastery is enlightened!'

The abbot was delighted and asked with great excitement, 'Master, please tell me which one it is, so I can offer them due reverence.'

The Zen master smiled, and said, 'I'm sorry, my dear abbot, I'm afraid I can't tell you that. But I'm quite sure that you and the others will find it out soon enough.'

Full of impatience, the abbot took his leave from the Zen master and hurried back to the monastery. As soon as he arrived, he summoned all the nuns and monks to the meeting hall and told them, in great excitement, about the Zen master's insight. At first all of them looked at each other in confusion, and then with curiosity – each one of them was secretly wondering who the enlightened one could be. After a short time, the abbot ended the meeting.

But at the very next meditation session, and at the following weekly meeting, there was a noticeable difference in how the nuns and monks treated each other. They greeted one another attentively, with esteem, because each one of them suspected that the other was the enlightened one. Just a few weeks later, a cheerful young guest arrived in the monastery. The chores were taken care of much quicker than before and the inhabitants of the monastery even started to renovate the parts that had fallen into disrepair. After a while, young novices started to come, seeking to be accepted into the community. Less than a year later the monastery was flourishing, and its excellent reputation had once again spread far and wide. The old abbot sat on his bench, happily watching all the productive activity and pondering gratefully upon the old Zen master's wisdom.

Questions to reflect on

- *In your opinion, how did the inhabitants of the monastery come to be at odds with each other?*

- *What change in the abbot's attitude led him to visit the Zen master?*

- *What effect did the Zen master's insight and recommendation have on the attitude and behaviour of the nuns and monks?*

In your opinion, how did the inhabitants of the monastery come to be at odds with each other?

It should have been the abbot's job (as a leader) to make sure the activities of the nuns and monks were aligned with a common sense of purpose and that a sense of community was actively created and experienced.

What change in the abbot's attitude led him to visit the Zen master?

He realised that he was no longer able to resolve the situation on his own. By seeking guidance from outside, he was taking full responsibility to do whatever he could to help.

What effect did the Zen master's insight and recommendation have on the attitude and behaviour of the nuns and monks?

It gave rise to a new, positive mode of interaction based on esteem. This released new energies, making trust and communal experience possible once again. From a psychological point of view, the narrative – the story the residents told each other – changed significantly to one that was positive and inspiring. Making narratives more positive and inspiring generally applies to every organisation and is a vital part of the leadership task. So, as leaders, in some way, we are also in the business of storytelling.

'The human person experiences his wholeness not in relation to one's self, but in virtue of his relation to another self.'

Martin Buber

Organisations and companies, at some level, can also be considered as a network where there is an exchange of information and energy. The medium for this exchange is communication. Therefore, an inspiring leader must, above all, be an effective communicator and facilitate purposeful communication within their company[40]. In a professional context, communication often takes place at the objective level and often, we are unaware of our own emotional and somatic levels, the space in which our stress and trauma finds expression, let alone those of others. And yet, both of these relationship-building levels are not only essential but become even more important in the virtual context.

Back in Chapter 2 we were invited to take a few baby steps towards experiencing meditation, and this book has tried to emphasise the benefits of reflective and contemplative exercises. Meditation is the practice of breaking our identification with our thoughts, allowing whatever we are experiencing – whether pleasant or unpleasant – *to simply be*. Meditation is not something we do; it is something we *cease to do*. We cease to be distracted by our thoughts[41]. This allows us to be open to whatever appears in our communication, and we can incorporate this awareness more and more into the fabric of our everyday lives.

The word 'communication' is derived from the Latin word *communicare*, which means to 'impart' something, to let someone 'take part' in something, to make something 'common' knowledge, or to 'unite'. The word 'commune', referring to a community of people dedicated to living their shared ideals, comes from the same root.

Human beings are social beings. We are the product of a union and during pregnancy we spend nine months in the closest possible union with our mother. We learn all of our important social skills through real-life relationships. This is why

40 On this subject, Peter F. Drucker, the father of modern management theory, said, 'Your first and foremost job as a leader is to take charge of your own energy and then help to orchestrate the energy of those around you.' On a relational, more human level, we can take the purpose of relationship and communication as being to alleviate suffering, i.e., to help the other in some way.

41 Sam Harris, in Waking Up, an app available in the App Store (see Chapter 1 exercise link).

effective communication, which by definition means being in a relationship with our communication partner, is vital for a fulfilling life, whether the contact is in person or in a virtual setting. Referring to Martin Buber's dialogic principle cited above, American sociologist Amitai Etzioni puts it succinctly as, 'The "I" needs a "we" to be'[42].

However, being socialised in a community and participating in communicative relationships does not automatically guarantee the ideal conditions for us to develop our personal communication skills. When we think about it, in our relationships we often find that the other person has blind spots or has a limited ability to co-regulate overwhelming emotions rooted in their childhood.

So, how can we establish a basis for more impactful communication, or even communication that allows healing, both for ourselves and the people around us? In many ways, this process resembles a mindfulness exercise. The first step is to make ourselves aware of the space in which our thoughts (mental level), feelings (emotional level) and physical sensations (somatic level) appear. In our fast-paced lives, without even noticing it, this space often becomes filled with information, experiences and the things we supposedly have to do. However, if we focus our attention on this inner space, as well as our thoughts, feelings and sensory input from our environment, we will also discover a type of generosity and perhaps even quietness. The more this quietness grows inside us, the more of ourselves we are able to give to another person. Of course, the opposite is also true – the smaller our inner space, the greater the likelihood that we will be overwhelmed by thoughts and emotions, and are then more likely to communicate in a reactive way. This means we are reacting to our own life circumstances, instead of truly responding to the other person. This diminishes our 'response-ability', or our capacity to give a genuine response. The simple fact of being aware of our inner space as a receptor for any kind of input allows us to be truly present. This means that the very first message we give back to the other person is our unconditional presence and our willingness to open this inner space to our conversation partner. In our practical experience of communicating with others, the ability to maintain this inner space is an acid test of our competence as communicators.

42 'In a relationship, one mind revises the other; one heart changes its partner. This astounding legacy of our combined status as mammals and neural beings is limbic revision: the power to remodel the emotional parts of the people we love, as our attractors activate certain limbic pathways, and the brain's inexorable memory mechanism reinforces them.' (Lewis, Amini & Lannon, 2007). Therefore, who we are and who we become depends, in part, on whom we love (Maria Popova, 2021).

In a second step, we look from the inside out. Like a musical instrument, we tune into the other person. This heightened awareness gives rise to empathy, and not only do we hear the words that are said, but also tune into the emotions and non-verbal elements that are exchanged – we become a sounding board that picks up vibrations and gives them back: 'I feel you as you feel me'. This is far more than pure empathy because it closes the circle between two people. In order to give this kind of attention to our conversation partner, we need to take our time. Instead of giving an answer straight away, based on the first association that comes to mind, we wait until our nervous system has attuned to that of the other person. This synchronisation enables both us and our conversation partner to explore each other's perspectives more deeply, by having greater access to a wider scope of resources and possibilities[43].

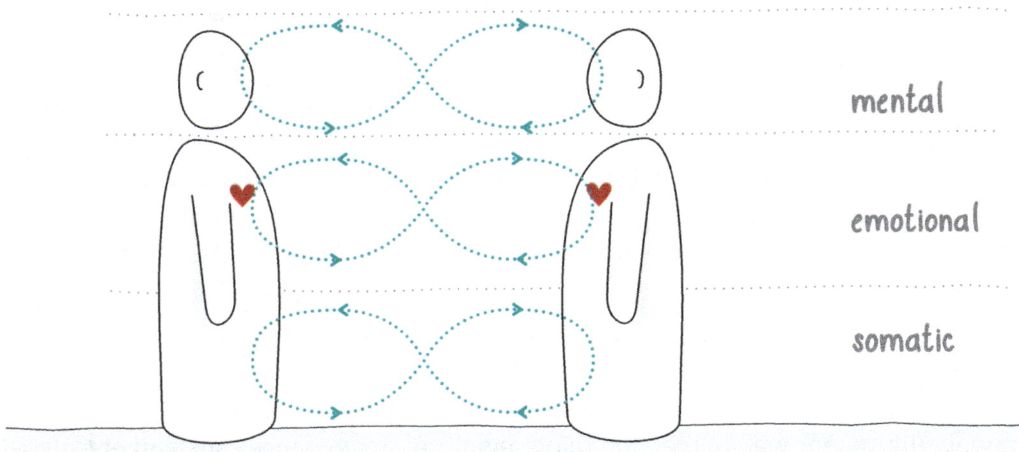

EMPATHY × AUTHENTICITY × ESTEEM = GOOD-QUALITY RELATIONSHIP

Figure 9: Being aware of our inner space, and determining the three levels within ourselves and in relation to others[44]

43 In the 2009 film *Avatar*, the expression 'I see you' is used as a greeting by the indigenous Na'vi people of the planet Pandora. Jake, a paralysed ex-Marine, uses an avatar which enables him to impersonate a Na'vi and embarks on a love affair with Neytiri, the chief's daughter. When Jake nearly suffocates, Neytiri sees him as a human being for the first time and uses the greeting 'I see you' – expressing a much deeper perception than that of mere sight.

44 The approach described is based on the client-centred communication techniques developed by Carl R. Rogers (2015), the 'Transparent Communication' course by Thomas Hübl (2009), and on Circling Europe's courses.

As well as taking time to become attuned to the other person, we also need to meet them in an appreciative way, i.e., with esteem. This creates a safe space in which the other person is able to acknowledge and co-regulate their emotions.

Accordingly, the most important contribution that we make to the communication process is to be present authentically as a person, long before we offer feedback in verbal form. In this way, we help the other person to find out how they perceive themselves. Once we have explored the other person's feelings, we can then share our own emotions.

And when it comes to emotions, there are two ways of determining whether the statement 'I feel' really expresses an emotion. We can pay attention to the word that follows it – terms like 'I feel good', 'I feel tired' or 'I feel hungry' clearly do not refer to emotions, and phrases such as 'I feel like' or 'I feel that' are also unlikely to express an emotion. We can test this a little further with a simple substitution; if we replace the word 'feel' with 'think' and the sentence still makes sense, then we are not expressing an emotion (Bradford & Robin, 2021). The more we nurture this ability, the more authentic we will be in that moment of communication.

In this context, there are a few basic but important rules that we should note.

› If we feel that our stress triggers have been activated, we should not try to give feedback to the other person because, in this scenario, it's not about the other person anymore, it's about us and our problems.
› Advice is not the same thing as feedback. During a conversation, the only source of information available to us is whatever is happening to us, or inside us, in the given moment. A piece of advice represents something that has worked well for us in the past, and that we are convinced would also be a good solution for the other person. But it is much more authentic, engaging and helpful if we share the perceptions that come to us while we are listening and give a 'live', spontaneous response to the other person's situation and the issues they bring up, rather than giving a response based on our past. Only by doing this do we open the possibility for something new to emerge for us both.
› And, last but not least, if we are feeling frustrated with our conversation partner, this is a good pointer to the unconscious, unintegrated parts of our own personality that we are projecting onto the other person (and perhaps more widely onto our view of the world). As soon as we can see, feel and be aware of what is really true in that moment, when our perceptions are com-

pletely focused on the other person and we are fully attuned to their situation and motivations, there is no room left for frustrations and disappointments, just understanding, empathy and compassion. And we cannot be disappointed – because disappointment is the unconscious result of an expectation that does not exist in the moment, and from which, therefore, true communication practice is completely free.

Conclusion

- **We**, as people, exist for and in relationships, and we **learn** our social skills in the practice of **relationships and communication.**
- To practise good communication, we need to be **aware of the space** in which thoughts, feelings and physical sensations manifest themselves, and we need to invite the other person into this space. When we do this, we are fully focused and attuned to the other person.
- This enhances our **response-ability**, or our ability to first be aware of our own feelings, and then respond to the other person.
- By acting **as a sounding board**, we gain a heightened perception of the other person.
- The quality of our relationship depends on the degree of **empathy, authenticity** and **esteem** that we express.

Exercises to go a bit deeper:

In the link you'll find instructions on how to take the first steps towards practising real communication.

→ www.zen-stories.com/en/zen-e

The end...

Or perhaps not?

We have reached the end of this book,

but the Zen stories keep on going...

Milarepa and the old man

Milarepa[45] had been searching everywhere for enlightenment but had never found it, until one day he saw an old man with a rucksack making his way slowly down a mountain path. Milarepa knew instantly that this old man was in possession of the secret he had been seeking so desperately all these years. 'Old man,' he implored, 'Please tell me what you know. What is enlightenment?' The old man looked at him, smiled, then let his heavy burden fall to the ground and stood up straight. 'I see!' cried Milarepa. 'You have my eternal gratitude! But may I please ask you one more question? What comes after enlightenment?' The old man smiled again, bent down and once again hoisted up the heavy bag. He placed it on his shoulders, adjusted his load, and went, laughing on his way.

45 Milarepa was one of Tibet's most famous yogis, poets and ascetics.

Questions to reflect on

› *How did Milarepa know that the old man was 'enlightened'[46]?*

› *When you are truly mindful, what changes in your actions and the impact you have on others?*

› *How can you judge the level of your own mindfulness or presence?*

46 In Zen Buddhism, the 'oxherding' picture sequence is often used to depict the stages of practice leading to enlightenment. The final picture shows the enlightened oxherder entering the marketplace, doing all the ordinary things that everybody does. He does not retreat from the world but shares his enlightened existence with everyone.

'If you think you're enlightened, go spend a week with your family.'

Ram Dass

Enlightenment is thought to refer to a 'final state' of deep being in which our true nature, free from any distorting constructs, is fully integrated with the flow of life itself from moment to moment. And whilst enlightenment, the essence of Eastern traditions, cannot really be captured by words, the Indian sage Nisargadatta Maharaj approached it elegantly by formulating it as a polarity: 'Wisdom tells me I am nothing. Love tells me I am everything. And between the two, my life flows.'

We spend a lot of time wanting to be happy – as if something were missing from our experience of the present moment. Despite all our efforts, there are only a few moments in our lives when we feel in our innermost souls that we have reached our goal. Most of the time, it feels like we'll never get there. This also has to do with our brain's ability to constantly learn things, and to restructure itself in the process (neuroplasticity). The search for meaning in our lives is a part of this everlasting process of seeking and becoming. We would all like to be able to tell ourselves a satisfying story about who we used to be, who we are now, and who we are going to become. Of course, it makes sense to do everything we can to assure ourselves of a fulfilled life and a meaningful career, to stay healthy and to nurture good relationships with those around us. But it is also frightening to think that nothing in the world is permanent and that we are at the mercy of fate.

As we have seen in this book, the stories we tell ourselves have power over us. But meditation can enable us to listen to the narrative with a quiet, centred intrinsic sense of clarity and serenity, without any sense of lacking something, allowing us to simply be aware of the moment. This is an even more profound discovery than finding our purpose in life. And yet, both of these insights are compatible. Whatever outward goal we strive for, it alone will never make us truly happy. We can only be happy in the present moment. Constantly making this discovery anew is the essence of meditation. The more we integrate this into our life, the more we will be able to perceive life in its unity, diversity, and uniqueness.

Milarepa and the demons

After wandering for many years, Milarepa returned to his old house in his hometown, only to find it occupied by demons. They ate the food from his stores, read his books and slept in his bed. They had completely taken over his home. During his travels, Milarepa had practised Zen Buddhism and had learned many things, but right now, he was not at all sure how to drive these devils out of his house. He knew that they were merely a projection of his own spirit, a symbol of everything that he didn't like about himself. But despite this, he couldn't come up with any practical plan.

So, he decided to teach them. He sat in a raised chair and spoke of how we are all one, and how everything in life is fleeting. He spoke of courage, empathy and vulnerability, and of how poison can also be a medicine. Nothing happened. The demons were still there. Milarepa soon ran out of patience and charged at the demons, intending to throw them out. They simply laughed at him.

In the end he gave up, sat down on the ground and said, 'I'm not going to run away, I'm going to stay here with you. And it looks as if you're not going anywhere, so why don't we all learn to live together?' In that moment all of the demons disappeared, except for one.

Milarepa thought, 'Oh my, this one is especially big and scary-looking.' He didn't know what to do, but he gave himself up fully to the moment. He went over to the demon, who was just opening its huge, terrifying jaws, and stuck his head inside and said, 'Eat me, if you want to.' As soon as he spoke, this demon also disappeared.

An afterword, but not an afterthought

Most of this book has been dedicated to shedding light on what I call the conditions that make us human, and following on from that, discussing the unconscious psychological basis of change and transformation.

This book pursues the question of how we can deal with everything that the acronym **VUCA** indicates – volatility, uncertainty, complexity, ambiguity – in a calmer and more conscious way, and to help others to do the same. VUCA represents all the challenges facing modern companies today, and the major upheaval this brings to our working lives. However, if, as leaders, we can learn to meet ***v**olatility* with an inspiring ***v**ision*, ***u**ncertainty* with a deeper ***u**nderstanding*, ***c**omplexity* with ***c**larity*, and ***a**mbiguity* with ***a**gility*, this will empower both us and our employees to discover a new and energising meaning of VUCA.

And this can transform our lives into a process of refinement through feedback, while at the same time allowing us to have a deeper experience and appreciation of living in the moment.

As Thomas Hübl, a modern mystic, so aptly put it, 'We're reading the book of life at the same time as we're writing it'. The closer the act of reading (i.e., experiencing life in its immediacy) comes together with the act of writing, the less we find the past to be an obstacle and the more aware we become of fully experiencing the world inside ourselves, while also being able to celebrate life on the outside.

'The world is full of magic things, patiently waiting for our senses to grow sharper.'

Y.B. Yeats

Thanks

We are always standing on the shoulders of the giants who came before us. It is our collective history – all of our inherited knowledge, wisdom, art, culture, science and technology – that makes it possible today for so many of us to realise more of our development potential than ever before. Similarly, this book is the product of many conversations with many different people over the years and insights from them, experiences and learning that life brought along.

I would like to thank all my family, but especially my wife Annika, and our children, Franzisca, Frederic and Jonathan, for their amazing support and for challenging me in ever inspiring and creative ways.

A big thank you to all of the team at aergon ag: Shirine Imoberdorf, Pierre Bachmann, Mélanie Huser, Annika Gartenmann, Iara Meili, and Jonas Erb, as well as our network of associates: Amanda Keller, Jörg Eugster, Renate von Grünigen, Sandra Haase, Maya Weber, Philine Behrendt and Rebecca de Regt. Without you, my understanding of friendship, collaboration and psychology would certainly be very different.

I would also like to thank Rachna Chowla and Verónica Fajardo for their meticulous and loving editing of this book, Guthrun Love for her perceptive translation from the original German into English, and Bernd Altenried, for his wonderful graphics and sensitive book design.

Finally, I would like to thank all my teachers, fellow travellers and friends who have been part of this journey of discovery: André S. Dreiding, Ernst R. F. Gesing, Chris Adams, Dimitrios Kalias, Sri Chinmoy, Manfred Kets de Vries, Sumantra Ghoshal, Martin Naville, Ulrich Thess, Christian Dreyer, John Clarkeson, Livia Dröge, Rolf Bixner, Winfried Berner, Felix Barber, Rupert Ley, Mary Barlow, Marc Pfitzer, Sandro Cornella, Franco Morra, Alice Sachova, Martin Tschopp, Daniel Ritz, Carina von Knoop, Nicola Rowe, Ulrik Schulze, Andreas Barner, Katrin Reuter, Hans Friedl, Michael Stanislawski, Klaus Pfaff, Beate Junginger, Samy Molcho, Joseph Lazenka, Markus Huppenbauer, Ruth Allamand, Tony Robbins, Philippe Johner, Markus Schmid, Thomas Gutzwiller, Anna Gamma, Dorothee Bürgi, Daniela Però, Patrick Looser, Carlos Salum, Friedemann Schulz von Thun, Fred Kofman, Michael Weitz, Alfried Längle, Gunter Schmid, Christina Hall, Jun Rong, Marco Kunz, Jamie Smart, Michael Neil, Andreas Bär, Adyashanti, John Demartini, Gita Belin, Richard Barrett, Andrew T. Austin, Rupert Spira, Esther Perel, Sam Harris, Paul King, Thomas Hübl, Rachna Chowla, Anna von Planta, Bernard Winterhalter, Erhard Widmer, Jan Rindlisbacher, Steven C. Hayes, and many more.

Bibliography

Antonovsky, A. (1997). *Salutogenese: Zur entmystifizierung der gesundheit.* (A. Franke and N. Schulte., Trans.). Tübingen: dgvt-Verlag.

Beck, D. E., & Cowan, C. (2005). *Spiral dynamics: Mastering values, leadership and change.* Chichester, United Kingdom: Wiley-Blackwell.

Boccia, M., Piccardi, L., & la Guariglia, P. (2015). The meditative mind: A comprehensive meta-analysis of MRI studies. *Biomed Research International, 2015.*

Bradford, D., & Robin, C. (2021). *Connect: Building exceptional relationships with family, friends, and colleagues.* New York, United States: Penguin Random House.

Bungay, S. (2011). *The art of action: How leaders close the gaps between plans, actions and results.* London, England: Nicholas Brealey Publishing.

Clear, J. (2018). *Atomic habits: An easy and proven way to build good habits and break bad ones.* United Kingdom: Avery.

Cook-Greuter, S. (2010). *Postautonomous ego development: A study of its nature and measurement.* Chicago, United States: Integral Publishers.

Dörner, K. (1986). *Neue praxis braucht neue theorie.* Gütersloh, Germany: Verlag Jakob van Hoddis.

Etcheverry, P. E., Le, B., Wu, T. F., & Wei, M. (2013). Attachment and the investment model: Predictors of relationship commitment, maintenance, and persistence. *Personal Relationships, 20*(3), 546-567.

Fæste, L., Hemerling, J., Keenan, P., & Reeves, M. (2014, November 3). Transformation: The imperative to change. *Boston Consulting Group.* Retrieved from https://www.bcg.com/publications/2014/people-organization-transformation-imperative-change.

Hamel, G., & Prahalad, C. K. (1996). *Competing for the future.* Watertown, Massachusetts, United States: Harvard Business Review Press.

Hazan, C., & Shaver, P. (1987). Romantic love conceptualized as an attachment process. *Journal of Personality and Social Psychology, 52*(3), 511-524.

Hübl, T. (2009). *Sharing the presence: Wo warst du bist jetzt? Wie präsenz dein Leben transformiert.* Germany: Kamphausen Verlag & Distribution GmbH.

Hübl, T. (2020). *Healing collective trauma: A process of integrating our intergenerational and collective wounds.* Boulder, Colorado, United States: Sounds True.

Johnson, B. (2014). *Polarity management, Identifying and managing unsolvable problems*. Amerherst, United States: HRD Press.

Kahneman, D. (2011). *Thinking, fast and slow.* New York, United States: Farrar, Strauss & Giroux.

Keupp, H. (2000). *Identität*. Retrieved December 16, 2020, from https://www.spektrum.de/lexikon/psychologie/identitaet/6968.

Korzybsky, A. (1933). *In science and sanity.* Lancaster, Penn. and New York: International Non-Aristotelian Library Publishing Company.

Lee, A., Willis, S., & Tian, A. W. (2017). Empowering leadership: A meta-analytical examination of incremental contribution, mediation and moderation. *Journal of Organizational Behavior, 39*(3), 306-325.

Lewis, T., Amini, F., & Lannon, R. (2007). *The general theory of love*. Retrieved from https://www.amazon.com/General-Theory-Love-Thomas-Lewis-ebook/dp/B000SEGHFK.

Lips-Wiersma, M., & Wright, S. (2012). Measuring the meaning of meaningful work: Development and validation of the comprehensive meaningful work scale. *Group & Organization Management*, *37*(5), 655–685.

Rogers, C. R. (2015). *Der neue mensch: Konzepte der humanwissenschaft*. Germany: Klett-Cotta Verlag.

Rooke, D., & Torbert, W. R. (2005). Seven transformations of leadership. *Harvard Business Review*, *83*(4), 41-57.

Snowden, D. J., & Boone, M. E. (2007). A leader's framework for decision making. *Harvard Business Review*, *85* (11), 68–76.

Stangl, W. (2022). *Das Wertequadrat von Paul Helwig*. Retrieved January 14, 2022, from https://arbeitsblaetter.stangl-taller.at/KOMMUNIKATION/Wertequadrat.shtml.

van der Kolk, B. (2014). *The body keeps the score: Brain, mind and body in the healing of trauma*. United States: Penguin.

West, M. A. (2021). *Compassionate leadership: Sustaining wisdom, humanity and presence in health and social care.* London, United Kingdom: The Swirling Leaf Press.

Wilber, K. (2000). *Integral psychology: Consciousness, spirit, psychology, therapy.* Boston and London: Shambhala Publishing.

Further reading

... more stories

Bastin, M. (2018). *Geh langsam, wenn du es eilig hast: Weisheitsgeschichten aus aller welt*. Germany: Coppenrath.

Bucay, J. (2013). *Let me tell you a story: Tales along the road to happiness*. United States: Europa Editions.

Gladwell, M. (2007). *Blink: The power of thinking without thinking*. Back Bay Books.

Schmid, T., & Uppgard, J. (2018). *Tanyas sammlung von Zen-geschichten*. (n.p.): Self-published.

Shafak, E. (2010). *The forty rules of love: A novel of Rumi*. London, United Kingdom: Penguin Books.

Shah, I. (2016). *Tales of the dervishes*. London, United Kingdom: ISF Publishing.

Watzlawick, P. (1993). *The situation is hopeless but not serious: The pursuit of unhappiness*. New York and London: W.W. Norton & Company.

Yalom, I. D. (2020). *Lying on the couch: A novel*. New York, United States: Harper Perennial.

... for a better understanding of your own psychology

Barrett, R. (2018). *Everything I have learned about values*. Morrisville, United States: Lulu Publishing Services.

Brooks, D. (2012). *The social animal: The hidden sources of love, character and achievement*. New York, United States: Random House.

Brown, B. (2018). *Dare to lead: Brave work. Tough conversations. Whole hearts*. London, United Kingdom: Ebury Publishing.

Eaglemen, D. (2012). *Incognito: The secret lives of the brain*. New York, United States: Random House.

Haidt, J. (2006). *The happiness hypothesis: Finding modern truth in ancient wisdom*. New York, United States: Basic Books.

Maté, G. (2010). *In the realm of hungry ghosts*. Berkeley, California, United States: North Atlantic Books.

Peterson, J. D. (1999). *Maps of meaning: The architecture of beliefs*. New York and London: Routledge.

Rubin, G. (2009). *The happiness project: Or, why i spent a year trying to sing in the morning, clean my closets, fight right, read Aristotle, and generally have more fun*. New York and London: HarperCollins Publishers.

... for more wisdom and inner guidance

Adyashanti. (2014). *The end of your world: Uncensored straight talk on the nature of enlightenment*. Boulder, Colorado, United States: Sounds True.

Bays, J. C. (2014). *How to train a wild elephant: And other adventures in mindfulness*. Boulder, Colorado, United States: Shambhala Publications.

Brown, B. (2010). *The presence process: A journey into present moment awareness*. Vancouver, Canada: Namaste Publishing.

de Mello, A. (1992). *Awareness: The perils and opportunities of reality*. New York, United States: Image.

Hawkins, D. R. (2015). *Transcending the levels of consciousness: The stairway to enlightenment*. Carlsbad, United States: Hay House Inc.

Judith, A. (2014). *Eastern body, Western mind: Psychology and the chakra system as a path to the self*. Berkeley, United States: Celestial Arts.

Kofman, F. (2000). *Conscious business: How to build value through values*. Boulder, Colorado, United States: Sounds True.

Krishnamurti, J. (1995). *Book of life: Daily meditations with Krishnamurti*. London, United Kingdom: HarperCollins.

Spira, R. (2017). *Being aware of being aware*. Oakland, California, United States: New Harbinger Publications.

Suzuki, S. (2020). *Zen mind, beginner's mind*. Boulder, Colorado, United States: Shambhala Publications.

About the author

Thomas Gartenmann has been working with leaders and individuals in organisations for over 30 years, enabling them to fully realise their own potential and that of their company – starting at the rational level, then shifting the focus increasingly to psychological and cultural aspects.

He was a Partner and Managing Director at the Boston Consulting Group and Head of the Healthcare Practice for Germany, Austria and Switzerland. Today, he is an executive coach, facilitator and entrepreneur in the field of cultural change and corporate transformation. With inspiration, humour and passion, he and his team at aergon help individuals and teams to unleash their potential and make their contribution to their community and to the world more meaningful and fulfilling. He sees himself as a catalyst for transformative change and firmly believes that stress and strain are not prerequisites to being creative and successful.

His natural curiosity and enthusiasm have led him to research and work across many different disciplines – philosophy, psychology, economics, chemistry and education. He is an accredited systemic coach with the Institut für Fort- und Weiterbildung in Germany and holds certifications in systemic, cognitive and behavioural psychology from institutions in the UK and the US. He is also a member of Thomas Hübl's core group.

He has a Doctorate in Chemistry and Education from the University of Zurich, and an MBA from INSEAD. Other sources of inspiration are meditation, singing and travelling. He lives near Zurich with his wife, their daughter and two sons. Now they have a dog as well.

Made in the USA
Coppell, TX
19 April 2023

15822246R00083